CW01669213

Richard and Mikey's Pilgrimage

Mikey Lear

Richard and Mikey's Pilgrimage
Published in 2010 by Capera

First Edition

Edited by Carrie Fishblood
Cover design and text formatting by Cornelius Lycett

www.caperapublishing.com

NORTH SEA
BALTIC SEA
IRELAND
KINGDOM of ENGLAND
GRAND PRINCIPALITY
OF LITHUANIA
KINGDOM OF
POLAND
THE EMPIRE
BAVARIA
KINGDOM OF FRANCE
SWISS CONFEDERATION
KHANATE OF THE CRIMEA
BLACK SEA
WALLACHIA
MOLDAVIA
OTTOMAN EMPIRE
KINGDOM OF SPAIN
PORTUGAL
SARDINIA
SICILY
NAPLES
CRETE
CYPRUS
FEZ AND MOROCCO
ALGERIA
BARBARY STATES
TUNIS
Abbreviations

I'm walking to Jerusalem

January 13, 2009

If you are wondering what my plans are about this whole going to Jerusalem thing, this is what I've got so far:

- I'm leaving on the 17th of January to get to Brussels and I suppose we'll start our walk from there on the 19th.
- I'm going with Richard Brittain who I met on Countdown. He's awesome.
- We're walking the whole way – unless we jack it in for some reason.
- Richard reckons it'll take between 6 months and a year.
- He also reckons we'll walk about 10 miles a day.
- We haven't planned a route and I don't think we're going to.
- We will probably be relying quite a bit on the kindness of strangers.
- It's a pilgrimage; there's no other reason for it.
- I'm going to take camping stuff, a change of clothes, a camera, a Bible and a tube of condensed milk as an emergency ration.

Brussels

January 18, 2009

I made it to Brussels by doing excellent hitching (thanks Craig) and I'm staying with Helene, a couchsurfing person.

Did you know that if you order an absinthe in a bar in France, the guy pours it over a teaspoon into a glass with two cubes of sugar in it and then very earnestly lights the cubes and patiently waits there while the sugar crumbles and the absinthe it's burning burns and then when it's all burnt up he pours water very seriously over the sugary gloop he's just made and into the glass? Well it's true. Definitely worth €3 even though absinthe is gross.

In other news, hitching from Dover port is ideal. It's like it has been designed for it. The only thing is that you should remember to get back to the vehicle you left your stuff in before it drives off, unlike I did. Luckily the guy was quite friendly and had pulled in somewhere to wait for me otherwise I'd now be without my pilgrim's staff (and also my tent and clothes, etc).

Belgium

January 26, 2009

Obviously I'd like to bang on for ages and ages about all our wacky adventures so far, and obviously you'd like me to but I'm probably going to run out of time. We're staying with a family who have generously let us sleep in their barn, above the totally alive cows no less, and I get the feeling that we're about to have dinner or something. Oh dear I seem to have wasted my precious time wittering away and now I'm being talked to. N'importe quoi. I'll carry on.

Walking

The walking has gone pretty well I reckon. Richard worked out how long each country should take before we left and it came out at two weeks for Belgium. After one week we seem to be halfway across it, so we're going OK. We're doing about 8 miles a day which is a little bit less than I thought we were going to be doing but Richard did some calculations and discovered that even if we carry on at the same speed we'll get there at the same time we had planned, slightly before Christmas.

Equipment

My new tent is totally excellent. It spurns water and I can even put it up in a barn (I tried that tonight). The same applies to my sleeping bag and my rollmat. I'm the most organised camper in town, which, since I'm in the smallest town in the world (yes, in the world, it's a fact) isn't saying loads.

I've just had a shower and that was the first time my therma-wicking-mohair-composite-ultralite left my body since I left home. It still doesn't smell.

Weather

It's mostly been pretty good. One time it did a bit of snowing but we didn't get too much in our beards and on the whole the walking has been quite pleasant. At night it has been pretty cold with a fair bit of shaking off of ice in the mornings to be done, but so far it hasn't stopped me sleeping or anything. And just about all my stuff is dry.

Richard was tempted to bring a samurai sword and binoculars and bird book but he left them all behind due to being too heavy. He has, though, brought a Belgian medal from the late 19th century just in case.

Sleeping

We've slept in our tents for five nights (one of which was in someone's garden), on a kind person's sofa (Richard) and bed (me) once, and broken into a bizarre little shed slash cabin we came across in the middle of nowhere. Richard ingeniously wiggled his hand through a gap below the window and undid the catch. If you're reading this and you're suddenly thinking to yourself (in Belgian), wait a minute, that's my shed, merci bien pour l'abri, et s'il vous plait, pressez pas des charges.

Tonight, as I may have mentioned, we're going to sleep above some cows in a barn.

Penniless

You may remember me saying that we were going penniless. That turns out to have been a lie because we're taking literally thousands of pennies. In fact about 20000 Euro cents – which in modern money is about two hundred pounds. I had failed to offload all my money before I arrived at Richard's house so forty or so is mine. And if some bet that Richard made comes off then he'll have another thousand pounds at his disposal at the end of the football season. Either way, we're being cautious with money.

People We've Met

This is just me, but I got to Richard's house from Helene's in a single hitchhike. The guy (I forgot his name) was going to the border of Belgium from Calais but because I told him I was going to Brussels, he took me there. To Richard's door, to be precise, via his mother's house to give me some (excellent) food. I tried to hide €30 in his car but he found it and gave it back to me.

On the next night we were busy putting our tents up in Huppaye after having asked everyone we could find for permission and a guy called Ghislain came along and asked us if we'd like to have a drink with him. As it happened we did like to but we had to attend to our fire which was halfway towards failing and so he upgraded his offer to us staying in his chalet. This we accepted, and as we were packing up our tents a couple of the people we'd met earlier came along on horses saying that there was an empty house we could use somewhere where there was heating and everything. Too late, we told them, and off to Ghislain's house.

He made us dinner and gave us wine and beer and told us about his ex-girlfriend who he is still in love with and various other interesting things. When he found out that we were going to Jerusalem he went off and found a book which had belonged to his father and before that to a saint (he didn't know which one). He said that sometimes his father would rip out a page and give it to someone, but only on very special occasions. Since he'd owned the book he hadn't given a page to anyone, not even his three sons, but if we prayed for him in Jerusalem he would give us one each. So now we really have to get there.

Later his son, Gilles, and a friend, Jean-Christophe (we seem to be in French Belgium) turned up with a bottle of fortified whiskey and Jean-Christophe told us, among other things, that his cure for depression (which had worked for him) was to hope for nothing. They also told us that if we came back in a year then we could have a big party with them and that also all our friends were invited from England.

Another person we met in a grocery store bought us a brioche and told us that we had to pray for him in Jerusalem. The brioche was excellent, and so there's even more pressure to get there.

In Modave we were putting up our tents and a guy called Dany came along and enquired in the way that people sometimes do. We mentioned about the fire we were planning to build and he gave some advice that I didn't quite follow and then reappeared an hour or so later. I was halfway through creating what would have proved to be an excellent inferno and he suggested that he had a better plan. Always keen to give other people their chance to shine, I abandoned my fire and we went to where he had a wheelbarrow full of wood and a blowtorch. He made a big pile and then blowtorched away and I'll have to say that what the method lacked in grace it made up for in results. The next morning he made us breakfast and a packed lunch and pored over maps and then came with us for our entire day's walk, all the way to Borlon. So he was our first co-pilgrim.

The people we're staying with tonight have opened their doors most hospitably to us. Although that's technically true, the place where we are sleeping is, in fact, doorless. You get in by climbing a ladder and bundling through a wall hole. Did I mention that Ghislain was a sort of trainee tarot card reader? Well he read our cards a few nights ago and made various predictions which didn't seem totally right, and tonight we've had our future told again by the lady of the house. Although she uses Jesus instead of cards. She said that we were going to be met in Jerusalem by a red haired relative and that I was going to be a primary school teacher after the trip. Also she said that when she wasn't too busy with the cows, she liked to heal people and that at some point (maybe last summer) she healed 687 people which seems like a pretty decent number to me. Unfortunately there was nothing wrong with us (she knew that) so she couldn't cure us. But we did have a go at milking the cows. Well I did, and Richard stood there awkwardly, occasionally getting sprayed with cowshit.

The Police

One night when it was snowing we had left it a little late to find somewhere to camp so we had to put our tent up without attaining permission from the landlord. Well he wasn't at home so it was partly his fault. A bit later, when it was dark, he turned up accompanied by two policemen very much in a manner that suggested unfriendliness. I dealt with it expertly by grovelling and pleading and apologising and almost crying and he said we could stay the night. The police, slightly fearing that they were redundant in the whole process, took our names and details from our passports and said that rules still applied to pilgrims and that if we left any mess they knew who we were. We left no mess.

Food

We're mostly eating bread and cheese with the exception of: a) when people give us food; and b) when Richard is hungry enough to think that my idea of just spending everything we've got to make the journey more exciting is a good one. And on Sunday Richard came back from the shop with some cheese, salami and four buns and said that he thought that that should be plenty for both of us for three days. I roundly disagreed and it was decided that he could try living on it for three days if he liked but that I would take €4,17 (the same budget) and buy what I liked. That was a Sunday and, the French being what they are (they're Belgians round here), there weren't many shops open so I didn't really have any food except for a waffle and a variety pack of salty nibbles that I found by the side of the road. And later we met Dany and he gave us a bunch of food and then we met the Benteins and they gave us food and Ghislain also sent us off with a selection of mini butters so I haven't spent any money since then and I still have a massive bag of stale bread to munch my way through.

The Route

These are some of the names I've written down: Teverun (R's house), Grez-Doiceau, Huppaye, Burdinne, Oteppe, Huy, Modave, Borlon, and Durbuy (pronounced Dooberry and renowned for being the smallest town in the world, and that's where we are now).

Richard

Here are some things that Richard has said:

– I'm not bringing a toothbrush. I don't really brush my teeth and they seem to be fine.

– What!? You're bringing toothpaste as well?!

– [on day four] The thing is, I don't actually like walking very much.

A Development

January 28th, 2009

This morning Richard decided that he'd had enough and that he'd given it his best shot and that he'd like to go home. So he got on a train. Now, to add to the list of hazards I have to deal with (hunger and cold) I also have loneliness. So far I'm not too miserable.

The Second Half of Belgium

February 2, 2009

Well Richard has left me and I'm still surviving. Without him around I definitely go faster, though I haven't done loads of working out how much faster. We were planning on getting to Germany on Sunday night and I got there on Friday at some point, so I have rocketed ahead of schedule. Just after Richard went home I came to a road which went uphill for about a hundred hours, and at the top there was a bunch of snow. I found out later that it hadn't snowed there for three weeks, so what I was seeing had just stayed there. Including in fields which faced the sun all day. No one told me about that! I thought the Ardenne was just another World War One battlefield, as I presume you did. Well it's not, it's French for, "Not mountains, but still surprisingly cold." And then, after a little walking, I discovered that I was on nothing less than a cross country ski course, complete with ski tracks. And then, as if that wasn't enough, I ended up on an actual ski slope with ski lifts. It wasn't functioning, but still.

On the plus side of all this sudden additional coldness, I was forced to seek shelter in Belgian towns and that is a plus because Belgians speak in a funny way. Here's my impression of them, but it won't be brilliant because my French isn't quite immaculate yet and also because I'm typing it, which often takes the edge off impressions:

Cesee nay pah une fed'meh. Voo dwar-vay shed'shay oon fed'meh.

Yes, it doesn't seem as hilarious written down as it does in my head. If you ever meet me and want to be amused remind me to do it with my real voice.

Although I didn't reach Germany until Friday I only really spent two more nights in Belgium because when they start speaking German it's Germany really. On one of those nights I slept in the kind of community room where six women would be liable to turn up and make jewellery (which they did while I was drying out my tent) and on the other I was the guest of a family who had the key to an equivalent room somewhere in their town but who thought it would be too cold. I slept in their garage and ate dinner with them which was chips. They had a deep fat fryer built into their kitchen. Now that's sensible. That means that whenever they want chips all they have to do is flick a switch and lift a lid. And they'll never lose it. If I were them I'd deep fat fry everything.

Germans

February 3, 2009

Do you want to know what Germans are like? They're like this: when I arrived in Germany I was a bit confused about where I was and I saw someone with a beard and a camera which was about a foot long and I thought, "That beard suggests a good knowledge of English," so I said, "Hey, do you speak English? Vous parlez Francais?" and he said, "Yah, vhichever you prefer." Then he and his friend instantly whipped out tons of maps and told me where we were and where I should go if I was insisting on going the route I'd outlined and where I should go if I wanted a more beautiful walk. Then I noticed that there was some chalk graffiti on the side of their car in Flemmish so I asked what it said and they chuckled and said, "Um, it's not very nice...it says, 'Go avay, man viv beard...and your Kodak.'" Which means that they were at least quatrilingual and also that Flemmish vandals are amusing and polite. Then later they drove past and offered me some money in case I didn't have enough.

No, that's a bad example; this is what Germans are really like: a bit later, when I was thinking about going to sleep and had put my tent up in a little village somewhere, it occurred to me that it might get cold in the night. I knocked on someone's door and asked them if I could borrow a blanket and they said, "Yah. But...do you vant a café?" And when I nodded vigorously (I was a little worn out at the time and I imagined putting tons of sugar in it – and also I imagined being able to sit down, etc) they said, "Unt soup? Yah – *Therese, mackmickmockmuck.* Come, come," and I was ushered in and then I sat and ate a massive meal which they seemed to have especially catered for, just in case about seven people of a normal appetite turned up. Then they gave me two pairs of socks and a thermos full of coffee and a jacket and a plastic bag full of snacks and fruit and whipped out loads of maps and checked them out for a bit. I thought that most of it was to be returned but it was all to take with me if I wanted it. I managed to persuade them that I had made a deliberate choice not to bring things like a thermos and gave it back, but seeing as how the hole in my socks had been sneakily expanding I accepted the socks. And the food, naturally; that's a sort of policy. They also wanted me to keep the blanket. And when I left, the mother, Therese, shoved €20 into my hand and because I always lose those, "No, no really, please I don't want it" battles, I ended up keeping it. Despite it being something of a policy not to accept money from anyone.

Yes, that's quite a good example of what Germans are like, but to give you a fuller picture: later that day (after I'd left Therese and her husband) I met a guy called Markus and asked him if there was anywhere in his village I could sit down and eat my lunch in the warm. After offering to drive me to the nearest town with such a facility and being politely turned down he negotiated eating with his family which I politely accepted. He also got out a bunch of maps and tried to give them to me and asked if I wanted to stay the night (it was only lunchtime, so I had to politely turn him down again). And he tried to give me a thermos. Can you imagine? When was the last time someone tried to give you a thermos? Probably never. I think for me it's never. Then within 12 hours two people tried to give me one. The exact 12 hours after I crossed the German border.

No, that's not such a good example now that I think about it. But this is quite a good one: in Bitburg I went into a bar to ask if anyone knew where the priest was so I could ask him if I could sleep in the church (as had been our habit, so far unsuccessfully) and had this conversation:

– Does anyone here speak English?

– [chorus of "a little"]

– I'm looking for the priest. Do you know where he lives?

– Why are you looking for ze priest?

– Um, I was hoping to sleep in the church tonight.

– No need, you can sleep in my gartenhaus. It's heated; you'll sleep well there.

– Oh. Gosh. Ok, thanks very much.

That was followed by Wilfred carrying on drinking and me trying to offload some of my €20 on buying a round and after quite a few "last drinks" – that's a local joke that I didn't totally understand at first but basically involves drinking a lot but calling each drink the last drink – I eventually succeeded in spending €5 of the twenty that had been weighing me down. In the morning he cooked me breakfast and packed up the leftovers for me (all delicious). Then later in the day I asked a group of walkers who didn't really speak English (because I speak German now – it's easy) if they knew where in the town I could eat my lunch and the guy said, "Lunch? Ah! Kommen," and briskly set off to a hotel restaurant. When we got there I looked a little unsure because I'd really intended on eating my breakfast leftovers (and some of the bread we'd been given in Belgium ages ago on the farm where we slept above the cows) and I didn't think they'd necessarily be cool with that but my new German friends said, "Du ist mein gast," or whatever it is that means, "Don't worry, I'm going to buy you a schnitzel," and I ate it with them either in silence or in mime (my German isn't as good as I previously made out). And the hotel gave me fruit for my snack bag and in the evening when I thought I'd get to eat some of my increasingly heavy load, the couple whose garden I was camping in gave me a couple of sandwiches and more fruit. I've never had so much fruit. I'm getting to the point where I might well have had my five-a-day.

And that's what Germans are like.

Penniless

Did I mention about this? I don't think I did. When Richard left, he took his money with him and left me with mine which came to €30. I was initially a bit unsure about carrying on alone and so was quite glad of having the money but I still liked the idea of going without anything. Anyway, while sticking to my principle of not accepting any money and spending as little as possible, I now have €35. I was given the twenty as previously outlined, then I bought some beer, also outlined previously, and then I gave a tenner to some church on Sunday. Afterwards, embarrassingly, the pastor (or whatever they have) tried to give me another twenty to find somewhere to sleep. I have spent nothing on food and I haven't once run out of food in my snack sack. I still have one of the buns that we were given on the farm over a week ago and tonight I ate with some more typical (see above) Germans so I didn't need to eat the packed lunch that the Americans gave me this morning (I'll probably mention more about the Americans later).

Comfort

Since Richard left me I have been warm or warm enough the whole time (quite often I get cold fingers but who doesn't?). I have been full a couple of times and never hungry. I've been entertained and surrounded by people most evenings and found the walking quite peaceful and not even boring – and certainly not depressing – like I thought I might. I have recently developed blisters on my feet on account of walking a little bit faster now than I did BR (Before Richard) but apart from that I find this whole thing totally delightful.

Today I walked along a path called (by the map anyway) Pilgersweg. That, for those not as fluent in German as I am, means, "Pilgrim's Way." Can you imagine how happy that made me? Furthermore, it was lined with little shrines with Mary in, quite often with a burning candle nearby. Brilliant.

Route

I'm literally inching along the map now if you have an appropriately sized map. If you have a desk globe type of map then I'm literally millimetering along and if you have a ginormous 1:2 map then I'm kilometering along. But no one has a map that scale. I don't know exactly how many miles I'm doing every day but it certainly feels like a lot more than the BR period. Probably it's just a bit more – but if I give you a list of places I've been to then you can work it out for yourself.

After Durbuy, and with quite large chunks of unintentional vagueness and no roads or forest tracks remembered: Bque de Fraiture (I can't remember what Bque stands for but this is the place with the ski lift), Ciereux, Rogery (where I stayed with the fryer owners), Beho, Aldringen, Stoubach (this is just in Belgium but as they speak German there I've counted it elsewhere as an example of Germany – possibly the German spelling is different), Leidenborn, Uttfeld, Lichtenborn (where Markus gave me lunch), Waxweiler, Merkishausen, Echtershausen, Bitburg (where I played the "last drink" game), Heidweiler, Salmtal, Osanns-Monzel (where I am now).

More Germans Warming Hearts

February 12, 2009

I know that my last entry was a little bit heartwarming but I'm afraid I haven't got anything different this time. Ideally I would have amusingly fallen in a swamp or at least suffered some kind of hardship, but all that's happened is another relentless barrage of generosity from brother Fritz. I don't want to subject your already overwarm hearts to unwelcome extra heat but I'm going to briefly outline the more mundane acts of hospitality that I've been the recipient of and detail a couple of the more extraordinary ones, so maybe only read this after visiting New Romney or trying to make a computer do whatever it's meant to do or whatever it is that particularly cools your heart.

When I was in Bitburg a while ago I thought about staying in the church, so I went along to the mass and it all looked highly probable until just at the end when suddenly I was homeless and it was 8 at night. I might also mention that I used this opportunity to offload another €10 which I noticed was more than anyone else gave. Anyway, I slept in the garden of an old couple and (no English spoken) they provided me with a couple of sandwiches and some fruit and a thermos of tea in the evening and again another couple of sandwiches in the morning.

Later I got to Heidweiler and generally poked around until I found some Americans talking in American. Naturally I was delighted so I tried to make friends with them and there's nothing easier than making friends with an American. They are army-dependants and there seems to be a lot of people in a similar situation, or at least there are tons of signs everywhere saying things like, "This place belongs to the army and if you come in here we're quite likely to shoot you in the head," or, "Speed limit is 70 for lorries, 50 for tanks," and you get the impression that Germany is still occupied. Anyway, they gave me pizza and hot chocolate and spoke in English and I slept in the garden. The next day two other American kids who were friends of the Kaisers (that's the first family, not the old-fashioned rulers) appeared by my tent clutching a selection of goods, specifically:

- three packets of peanuts
- a triple pack of chewing gum
- a hunk of Rittersport (which is chocolate)
- a little paper cross which says "Jesus Loves You" on it

I managed to convince them that I didn't want the chewing gum, which completely baffled Carter. He assumed that I must have meant that I didn't know what to do with it, so he kept explaining it until eventually he took it back and started eating it. He also said things like, "I guess you get to talk to God a lot," and, "We'll be praying for you the whole time." Sonja, the mother of the first family, also gave me a little book about, "What the Bible really says." It turns out to be a Watchtower publication, though they never mentioned being Jehovah's Witnesses at the time.

Then, after walking along the Pilgersweg, I stopped at a house and said words to the effect of, "Can I put my tent in your garden?" and they said words to the effect of, "Of course! Come and have dinner with us and generally make yourself at home." And later Herr Zimmer made me a photocopy of a star map. I've been really excited about using it every night since but it has always been too cloudy.

Sometimes I don't have much to do when it gets dark except watch the stars and I thought it would be a good idea to learn what they're all called and stuff. But I'm afraid I'll have to learn it all in German because that's all I've got. No Canis Major for me, only Grosser Hund.

I was treated similarly by the Conrads, and once Christina (the mum) had put her swarm of children to bed we sat down to the classic Catholic evening pastime of drinking wine and singing hymns. Christina was on guitar and Hubert was on maracas and they specially chose songs which I would understand. And they also explained how to use a rosary and gave me one and printed out a thing with the Hail Mary on it because it was a bit embarrassing that I didn't know it and washed my clothes and tried to give me more clothes because my jeans were worn out and gave me some money. I tried to refuse, really I did, but eventually I said, "Look, I'll only give it to the next church I go to," and Hubert said, "You can give it to a certain church in Jerusalem if you still have it then." So we agreed on that. Now I have €45 which is fifteen more than I started with, despite having given away twenty to churches and spent five on beer.

Another time Anne, from Anne's Bistro in Rhaunen, gave me a sandwich and a coffee and an energy drink and some woman in a shop where I filled up my waterbottle gave me a bag of peanuts. I stayed in the gartenhaus of Gudula and Alfons and they gave me dinner and breakfast and also a bottle of wine from the region. A crazy woman drove past me and stopped and tried to force me to accept a lift and then told me I could stay with her or with her brother and jabbered away in the middle of the road for ages and gave me her phone number in case I needed anything. The people I met last night gave me, without asking if I wanted it, half a roast chicken and, in the morning, breakfast and a packed lunch including two massive sausages, cake in a Tupperware box and a tin of somethingwurst (wurst is great, and even though it's never immediately obvious that it isn't catfood, it always tastes excellent).

Apart from that, very early one morning while I was still in my tent I heard someone calling me; it turned out to be a lady called Pietra who had brought me some coffee in a thermos and a packed lunch of sandwiches and homemade cake. I suppose she had seen my tent and just decided to bring me food because people in tents need food.

I also camped in a dentist's field (which weirdly also contained a pony – I asked why they didn't just have fish like normal dentists but apparently dentists don't have fish round here), and someone came along with a bag in her hand and said, "Mockmack, essen [that means meal, or eat, I've found], orangen, apfel, oi [eggs], wurst [sweet sweet wurst], brot, unt chocolate, mockmackmick zie! Zie! ZIE!" I can't remember what the last bit was exactly but she was holding money out at me and it was obvious that she was saying, "Take it! Take it! TAKE IT!" and I artfully managed not to by saying, "Ish haben, nein, danke, zeer freundlish, danke, nein, ish haben, danke" loads of times. She can't have had any way of knowing who I was or why I should get any food. The eggs were warm still.

And finally, at least in this litany of niceness, I asked directions from a friendly looking ancient man who was standing in his doorway and he pointed the way (no English) and then said, "Mackmick café mack essen," and ushered me into his kitchen and set about dodderingly making me a cup of hot chocolate and heating up a massive panful of soup. He used a stick to get around with and had his sofa raised up a foot or two so that he could sit on it without really bending his legs; he generally behaved as if he were probably old enough to have been involved in the war except that instead of being anything like what you might imagine Nazis to be like he just kept putting food in front of me and saying, "Essen. Essen alles." Also he said, "Jawohl" like real Germans are meant to.

Route

From Osannes-Monsel, I went to: Irmenach, Rudolfshaus (or possibly Burschied), Rhaunen, Sienhachenbach, Reiffelbach, Dielkirchen, Marienthal, Donnenfels, Marnheim, Monsheim, Worms, Heddesheim, and now I'm in Heidelberg. I've sadly lost a lot of the millions of maps I've acquired along the way, but anyway they couldn't reproduce the hills I've accidentally walked up or the pointless circuits I've taken without realising it. You'll just have to imagine them.

Other Things

February 13, 2009

Kit

I have now pretty much used everything I brought with me. I haven't used the corkscrew or the toothpick or the tweezers on my penknife but I have used my penknife so that was worthwhile. The last thing to be used was my inhaler which I just brought to please my family but turned out to be useful because I'm allergic to more than one place on earth it seems, and I went to the other place. Also that stupid roll of plaster stuff which was obviously pointless came in quite handy when I started developing blisters. Also you'll be desperately interested to know about the state of my undergarments, I imagine. So I'll tell you.

Well I started wearing white pants which was an error, but then when I stayed with the Americans they gave me a new pair of pants which are both: a) as long as trousers; and b) definitely pants and not trousers. Since then I have been wearing them and they are much cleaner on account of being khaki. Every so often someone offers me a jumper or something and I have found two hats by the sides of the road, so I reckon that in not long I'll be totally wearing given stuff.

Pain

Before Richard I basically felt no pain because we were going at Richard's natural speed which is slower than mine. Immediately After Richard I sped up and that was fine but a couple of days AR I developed blisters, as you would. On my left foot I had a good one on top of my big toe which never quite joined up with the one underneath my big toe. Anyway, they've all gone now, or at least today I walked for more than 30 clicks and the only thing that bothered me was my back which was more of a background pain when my feet were blistering but now has more of a voice.

Bunyan

So far I haven't faced any hobgoblins or foul fiends. I haven't had to show bravery in the face of a lion, nor fight a giant. In fact no one so even besets me round with dismal stories. The worst that could be said from Bunyan's poem is that I've had to endure a bit of wind and weather, but not as much as I would have done in England, I don't think. Still, if anyone got close enough they could hear me singing it every so often. It's quite a cheery song.

The Middle of Germany

February 23, 2009

German

Here are some useful German words I've learnt:

Stick – schtock
Walk – wander
Map – karte
Path – weg
Bike – rad
Guest – gäst

Book – büch
Kind – freundlich
Walking stick – wanderschtock
Footpath – wanderweg
Map with footpaths marked on it – wanderkarte
Map with bike paths and footpaths on it – radwanderkarte
My book, which I have written people's names and addresses in – wanderbüch (I produced it once and someone said, "Ah! Ein wanderbüch!" as if they were not only commonplace but so ordinary as to require a single word to describe them)
Friendly to bikers – radvererfreundlich (or something like this, I've seen it on a sign)
Hospitable – gästfreundlich. Gästfreundlich is a word that was invented to describe Germans.

Gästfreundlich

In Eberbach the Leytzes, an evangelich Pfarrer (which I think means protestant vicar) and family gave me loads of birthday food (it was Ellen's birthday – I gave her a hat which I happened to have spare) and I stayed in their gartenhaus. Then in Limbach Pfarrer Klok (a Catholic priest) let me stay in the jugendhaus, which I think is a sort of youth centre. If RB had been with me we could have played table football but instead I read about what Jehovah's Witnesses believe.

I quite often stop when I'm walking to rest, and when it's cold (which it quite often is) I quite often go into a café or a gästhaus and say, "Ich bin ein wanderer. Ich bin [impression of being tired]. Ich habe kine geld. Setzen? Ist ok?" and instead of saying the German version of, "This is a place where people swap money for drinks and the seats are sort of part of the service. If you have no money then it's totally inappropriate for you to just come in and sit down. Sit outside, there's a floor there which is open to the public," they generally say, "Ja, ja," then a few seconds later, "Dranken?" and I say again that I have no money and then they give me a coffee or something. And sometimes a meal. Well in Seckach I went into a café and I wasn't given a meal but I ate the last of my bread from my snack pack and I noticed that I was down to half a tin of würst. It occurred to me that I could end up with no food in my bag for the first time and that this was the first time I'd had no bread. As I was noticing the waitress gave me a loaf of bread. And then someone else bought me a milkshake (after I'd refused her money) and then someone else gave me a map (which was useless to me but hard to refuse) and then the waitress gave me a baloney (at least I think it was a baloney).

I later met the Pittners in Hergenstadt who were all prepared to let me sleep in their wagon (for some reason they had a wagon) but then they thought maybe I'd like to sleep in their house instead and I consented, and we had excellent würst and cheese and bread. Germans eat lots of bread and cheese and meat type meals. Breakfast, for example, is almost always bread and cheese and meat with the option of jam as well, and there's normally another meal in the day which is the same. And they eat it off a wooden board, like a chopping board.

After breakfast with the Pittners their son walked with me towards Jerusalem for about a kilometre. He was the third person to come with me for a section.

I also stayed with Heike and Peter in Leuzendorf and I learnt a new thing about German hospitality. It seems that giving a stranger a meal is totally normal here, but that letting a stranger sleep in your house is pretty odd. When I met Heike, she came out of her house and stopped whatever it was she was up to to walk round the town with me and help me find a place to sleep. After a few unsuccessful attempts and an offer to drive me to somewhere and a lot of discussion with Peter, eventually she said that I could stay in their barn, but she was obviously distressed by the idea. I examined the barn, and it had some hay in it which I could put my tent on and I said it was excellent and thank you very much and she became even more distressed and then after more discussion with Peter said, "No, I'm ashamed to have you sleep here, you can sleep in our house." Which seemed like a much better idea to me, but she was still distressed and eventually said, "I'm not very comfortable having a strange person in my house." I gave her my passport and she inspected it and that made her happier, but it occurred to me that lots of the other people I've met have been really generous in several ways while at the same time not inviting me to sleep inside. I don't understand that at all – the way I see it, they'll get their floor back if I sleep on it, but they'll never see their food again if I eat it. But it works out well for me because I love food a lot more than I love being inside. And I have an excellent tent.

Last night I went to Leutershausen and on my way to the church (to ask about a place to sleep) I saw a kebab shop and I thought I'd ask in there, mostly because I wanted a kebab. Luckily for me Ceyhun, the best dönerman in the world, was superfriendly and gave me a kebab and then another kebab and then some chips and phoned people and soon I had the gemindehaus for the evening and a stomach full of greasy goodness. He said that he ate at least one kebab every day and referred to himself as the Dönerman a lot, making me think of him like a superhero. He also hugged me. It kind of made me want to work in a kebab shop.

Money

I am currently winning my battle to have no money. At the moment I am carrying €20 which I owe to a church in Jerusalem, so it's not mine. I suffered a mild set-back when I was in Limbach because I went to church. As the priest had generally organised my shelter and given me dinner, he knew about my pilgrimage and thought it would be a good idea to share it with the congregation and also to get a fairly embarrassed altar girl to translate a message of goodwill for me. After the service I went and said thank you to the girl and while I was talking to her one of the punters shook my hand but he did the old five-Euros-in-the-palm routine which I wasn't prepared for and, even now, having thought about it, I still have no idea how to avoid taking palmed money. So I took it.

I've generally been giving my money to churches, but it occurred to me that that's quite a boring way to use it, especially since it is meant as a present. So I bought cake with my last fifteen Euros. I went into a bakery and handed over the money and said in an expansive and generous way, "Give a piece of cake to anyone who comes in here until the money has run out!" Then I said it again a few times in different ways until I got the impression that the girl behind the counter probably understood. She was totally baffled and not nearly as impressed as I had hoped she would be, but that's what you get from trying to impress people with cake. I still think it's a good idea though, so if I end up with more palm-money I'll probably spend it on cake, not church.

Also, I said before that I gave more than everyone else to the collection in church. I found out recently that if you are a member of church in Germany then you get taxed. You have to de-register yourself at the registry office to become a non-member and then you don't have to pay church tax but also you can't baptise your children or get buried by a priest or whatever.

Route

After sleeping just outside Heidelberg in my tent in a little patch of non-snow under a tree (this is after it started snowing but before it got cold), I belted it along the Neckar to Eberbach in one day which is probably the furthest I've managed so far and might have been 20 miles. Bike paths along rivers are fast and easy. Then I left the Neckar to go to Unterdielbach, Mülben, Balsbach, and then stayed in Limbach in a Jungendhaus. Then Heidesbach, Seckach, Adelsheim and Hergestadt where I stayed with the delightful Pittners. Merchingen, Ballenberg, Krautheim, Dörsbach, Hohebach and I slept in a Gemindehaus, which I think means town hall. Ailringen, Zaisenhausen, Bartenstein, Eichswiesen which, due to the constant snowing, had a perfectly good road going into it and no road coming out so I had to do a full ü-turn and go back to Riedbach (where I met the Zimmermans and ate a huge quantity of food), then Shrozburg and Leüzendorf where I stayed with Heike and Peter. They, and a few other people, insisted that I went to Röthenburg on the basis that Japanese people always seem to, and then I started heading in the right direction again (for the first time in a couple of weeks) to Geslau, Lauterbach, Buch a. Wald, Jochsberg and Leutershausen along the Altmühlweg bike path, which had been cleared by superefficient German snow removing machines. I stayed here in the Gemindehaus and was looked after by the best Dönerman in the world, Ceyhun. Thencly, still following the excellent Altmühlweg, Görscheim, Neunstetten, Herrieden (where I ate a work of exquisite beauty, created by Paul Limbacher), Selingsdorf, Thann, Großenried, Mörlach, and Ornbau where I am now. I was offered the chance to stay here for two nights and yes, I took it. So I'm having a day off and there's nothing you can do to stop me.

God

February 24, 2009

Before I left, James (my vicar at home) kept talking about counting your blessings and sometimes he mentioned trying to see bad things as a blessing. Or looking for the blessing in something which seems bad. The Muslim guy who drove me to Richard's house told me an Arabic phrase (which I've now forgotten) that he translated as, "Thank God – it means you thank God when it's good and you thank God when it's bad." It is very easy at the moment to thank God. Everything around me is good. The people I meet are all good. The food I eat is all good. The weather is always good. Sometimes the weather is horrible and then I think to myself, "Thank God when it's good and thank God when it's bad," and look for a blessing and there are always loads. There are all kinds of good things about blisters and cold wind and a wet tent. You can't really enjoy not having blisters in quite the same way if you haven't recently had them. My feet are quite hard and callused now, and I find that very satisfying. It's easy to thank God for my blisters. It's even easier to thank God for the other things that I'm constantly surrounded by. The snow, the sun when it's out, the stars when it's clear, the food that I'm given, the people I meet. I think having no money makes it particularly easy to see God.

Every time I eat food that someone has given me I tell them it's delicious. Probably some of it is kind of average and if I'd paid for it in a restaurant I'd think, "Hm, that was a bit of a rip off," but that thought isn't available to me. I have no reason to expect any food now, and that makes everything taste good. In the Lord's Prayer there's a bit which goes, "Give us this day our daily bread," but I don't say that now. Instead I say, "God, you are my daily bread," which probably doesn't make sense to anyone except me. It sort of means that if I don't get any more food, I accept that and I'm grateful for the food I've already had. It just seems too much to ask for more.

People keep asking me why I'm doing this pilgrimage and I keep saying I don't know and that I hope I'll find out. Maybe one of the reasons is to learn to expect less. If I expect food and comfort and warmth then it won't seem like a gift from God when I get it.

The third chunk of Germany (almost in Austria)

February 28, 2009

Instead of Bonfire Night in Germany they have Karnival, which is a bit like Mardi Gras in that it happens before Lent, but it starts, as far as I can tell, just after New Year. All the time I've been walking I've been bumping into things which are for Karnival; some towns take it more seriously than others. Ornbau, where I stayed with Christian (and from where I last wrote) takes it pretty seriously, and on the Thursday that I was there there was a thing which translates as Oldwomanskarnival which is basically the same as a fancy dress themed night in the pub except mostly for women. We went. I was an angel and Christian was a witch and his mum and aunts were all black people, very much in the minstrel style. He didn't see what all the fuss was about when Harry dressed up as a Nazi.

Then on the Saturday little urchins go from house to house cracking their whips and playing accordions in exchange for booze and everyone builds their parade vehicles (which are dragged around by tractors or quad bikes); on Sunday they all drive round the town throwing sweets at the onlookers dressed up as whatever they fancy and drinking a lot. Then they take their vehicles apart and on Wednesday they go to church. I didn't see all of that in the same place, but I did see the parade in Kipfenberg and I went to two Ash Wednesday services in different places.

Apart from Karnivalling, I have of course been accepting hospitality in the usual manner. I don't want to give the impression that all Germans are spectacularly nice because some of them aren't really. But I never really spend that long with the less nice ones. If I feel like what they're saying is, "Not In My Back Yard," which they quite often are, I say, "OK, danke," and move on. Which means that I have forgotten about them a few seconds later whereas the people who are nice to me I still remember.

About those people, one of them was a family of bakers who had a constant supply of bready goods and who fed me with some of them and gave me a kilo or two to take with me. They sort of made me want to have a bakery. Another was a couple who spoke no English but who had solar panels. Whenever I see solar panels on roofs (and there are a lot of them around here) it always makes me happy and I always assume that the people living there must be good and nice.

Actually, what normally happens is that they are old which means they don't speak English so I haven't really been able to find out about whether it's worth it or not. Anyway, this couple let me sleep in their garage type place and gave me a meal of bread and smoked bacon, but the kind that you only see in foreign countries which is mostly fat. I had to closely watch the father so I knew what to do. You cut off the rind (not the fat; that would leave you with nothing) with a massive wooden-handled hunting knife and then cut thin strips of fat off and eat them. Then you eat some bread. Luckily I've spent a bit of time overcoming my feelings of disgust towards unusual eating habits because otherwise it wouldn't have been delicious. But I love fat these days.

When I arrived in Kipfenberg I knew that they had their parade that day so I asked someone where I could sit down for a few hours without spending any money. He instantly got out his wallet and I persuaded him to put it away and walked into town and found a pub. The pub people were wearing costumes and being jolly and gave me a drink of some sort and then they said, "Do you know this man?" pointing at the swinging door, "he said to give you €10." So I earned a tenner which I later spent in the same pub on shots of weird Austrian schnapps.

I also stayed with Herbert Früwirth who has a Praxis in Wettelsheim. You may wonder what a Praxis is, and having done quite an in-depth investigation I'm still not totally sure. Certainly it involves some medical procedures but I couldn't say whether he is Herr Früwirth or Doktor Früwirth, though I suspect it's the former. Among other things he had a sort of lava-lamp which had spinning water in it which was designed to suck up elektrosmoke (though I haven't checked, I presume the English for this is 'electrosmoke') which is produced by computers and other machines. He also had a big canister which he ran his water through and which had lots of little tubes running round inside it which turned the water from dead (because it had been travelling in a straight line in a pipe for ages) into alive (like water in a stream), and I had a bath in said water for 35 minutes (I was allowed between 35 and 40) at a temperature of 38 degrees. And he did a health check on me which involved wearing a pair of headphones (which I think both picked up my frequencies and also gave out some frequencies, electrosmoke being sucked up by the 7-colour lamp) while we both looked at his laptop which kept producing maps of different parts of my body with different areas marked as being ill for some reason. He discovered two different viruses which he gave me pills for (with labels like €15 on them) and zapped certain bad bits with his mouse with the pleasing result that they got better. After zapping the viruses he took a closer look at my cells and zapped some of my chromosomes and then, as if that wasn't enough, he zapped the individual links between the DNA strands. It went slightly outside my realm of biology at that point but he managed to actually strengthen the bonds between the atoms in the molecules of G, T, S and A (or whatever those four molecules are). I felt both baffled and pleased. And every time he did a different area of my body he checked the frequencies, compared the frequencies with what they should be in a healthy body, worked out the difference and blasted a bottle of water (alive) with it. Then at the end he gave me the bottle of water and I'm to take 10 drops a day of it and it'll strengthen all the weak bits.

When I left he gave me a quick physics lesson including lots of stuff I'd been taught in school about atoms and electrons and such and then some slightly surprising diversions from the traditional theories, like that the sun does not, in fact, produce any heat or light. "Zat. Is A Beeg. Lie!" is what he said about that: apparently the sun just reflects an even bigger light / heat source which is in the middle of each galaxy and also explains the shape of galaxies (which is a bit like a flying saucer). The long and the short is that probably I'm going to start getting a lot healthier, although I felt pretty healthy before I met him.

When I left he produced €60 and told me to take it and I artfully refused for a bit until he started to get angry and that, combined with him saying that it wasn't for fun but for if I met a holy person who needed it or something, made me accept it. I spent fifteen on cake at the next cake shop and now I'm down to €65.

Kit

I have quite a strong feeling that everyone I know wants to know about my kit, though I sometimes have doubts about that. Well in this week's kit spotlight are the neckerchief and the stick. My neckerchief has proved useful for the following things:

- keeping nose warm
- keeping hair out of eyes
- keeping head warm (but not as warm as a hat)
- stopping breath from putting out a fire
- wiping nose
- cleaning inside of tent
- carrying little bottles of booze which were given to me in a bundle on my stick

My stick has less uses but is constantly handy. It has shrunk by at least an inch since I started, which I know because I made a mark on it which has now been ground up. Also I went to church the other day and they were singing a song which had the word Pilger in it, so I asked for a translation and someone told me it meant that Jesus is like the pilgrim's staff. Isn't that excellent? Well I was pleased.

Begging

When I started people asked me how I was going to get food and because I hadn't really thought about it much I said, "Well, we could beg." This prompted my friend Rory (who I also met on Countdown) to effectively dare me not to beg. He said it in a much more spiritual way, but the general gist was, "You'll be much cooler if you don't beg," and I have borne that in mind. I haven't asked for any food except once by accident (which was a result of the German words for "apple" and "waste" sounding the same – I ended up with three apples), but I do always put myself in situations where people can give me food, which is pretty much the same if you ask me. Like I deliberately put my tent up in the middle of a town rather than in the forest somewhere, thinking that someone might offer me food.

Route

I have basically sailed along the Altmühl to the Main-Donau-Kanal and now I'm going along the Danube (which they call the Donau round here) (and which isn't as blue as everyone says). I should be going along here for a while now and might even be in Austria by the end of the week.

I didn't literally sail, by the way.

Bunyan

Today I went into a restaurant and asked to sit down without buying anything and the playful Italian owner came out and said, "But you will sing us a song!" and I warned him that I wasn't a very good singer and he trumped that by saying that I could have everything for free if I sang and then I remembered that I'd been singing 'To Be A Pilgrim' every day for the last month so I gave the whole place a pretty mighty blast of that and earned my lunch. He didn't ask for the second verse and nor was it given.

Weather

It snowed a while ago and I did see some actual skiers skiing a few days back but now the snow is pretty much gone. There are still hunks of it around but for the last couple of nights I have slept in my tent and been perfectly comfortable. My new problem is wet, which seems to be everywhere and is hard to get out of my tent. It feels like winter is coming to an end.

The End of Germany (really this time)

March 6, 2009

I've made it to Passau which is on the Austrian border – and what better way to celebrate than with a spot of low-quality humour? Here's a joke I invented during one of the long periods in which I have time to think about important things: After walking for a long time, I was tired and looking for somewhere to sit down when I saw a bench! I was laufen all the way to the Bank.

Lent and Beer

On Ash Wednesday I was tucked up in my sleeping bag eating some chocolate nut treats when I heard the church bells going like crazy and after a while I realised that probably there was a service I could go to (my second of the day). They do the bells so well around here that I was one of the first people to arrive and then, to my delight, it turned out to be a service where the men sit on the right and the women sit on the left and everyone does a rosary together. The men say the first half of each prayer and the women say the second half, and then the roles get reversed for the next decade and there are various other complications to keep you on your toes. After a while I worked out what was going on and could even join in (in English) because I've been practising my Hail Mary. When we were getting to the end of our rosary the bells went again, more people arrived and the real service began with the ashing of the forehead, etc. I'd gone to the special early bit for the really keen.

Also, I think Ash Wednesday was the day I arrived in Bavaria because from then on, and without any kind of planning on my part, I had at least one beer every day for the first week of Lent. It just kept flowing towards me, and then someone said, "It's normal, you're in Bavaria," and that seems to explain everything. They always drink beer from not very far away and it always seems to be called "Hell" which I think means "light" or something. One of the beers I was given was called "Spital Hell." Not for export, I think.

Regensburg

After I last wrote I started to leave Regensburg by heading back to the Danube and someone noticed me and said that I could stay with him if I liked and he seemed friendly so I said, "Yes why not," and he said, "Ok, in you get," (he was in a car) and I said, "Well, no, I'd like to do it all by foot if you don't mind..." and he said that he was going in the wrong direction so maybe that would be ok, and maybe I could get a bus but I refused and said I'd walk. Well it was quite a severe distance to be walking in the wrong direction. Probably 5 miles or so, but luckily halfway there I met a bunch of youths who were sitting around a fire with two crates of beer and a bottle of whiskey and they told me the direction to go and then said, "But, will you have a beer?" and then we became friends and I ditched the other man and slept at Leo's house instead and ate most of his food. I get the impression that wherever I go I eat most of my hosts' food. Then in the morning I walked back again, and generally got the feeling that I knew Regensberg quite well by the end of it.

Most of Austria

March 18, 2009

I've been in Austria now for ages and you're probably wondering what Austrians are like. Well, they're like this: when I first got into the country I knocked on someone's door and asked them if they knew where I could put my tent and they said, "Yes, there," and then, when I'd unfurled my tent, they said, "Or you could sleep inside if you like." And then, because they'd already eaten, they made me dinner and gave me cake and played football with me and Jan, one of the two sons, decided to come with me for 10km the next day and even though it was raining and not a particularly nice day for walking he did indeed come. Or, to put it another way, the next night I asked the same question to someone else and he gave me an almost identical answer except that he didn't come with me the next day and he had a sort of B&B which I stayed in and I had dinner with his parents who spoke no English so as you can imagine mein Deutsche is sehr gut jetzt, oder? I think if you say, "Oder?" at the end of a sentence it means "Innit?"

Or to put it in a variety of other ways, the bakery and pub owners in Over Austria have fed me without being asked. Or you might say that Austrians are a bit like Germans which I suppose isn't massively surprising. Except I have a feeling that the hospitality I have been accepting has become a bit more practical. Less bags full of a selection of fruit and chocolate treats and more, "Do you need bread? Here, take some bread."

However, since I reached Under Austria I have altered my survival policy a little. The bike path took me past a supermarket and the carpark was empty and there was a dumpster sitting there and I thought, "Hmm, I wonder if they leave food lying around in dumpsters in this country like they do in England. And it was so easy to go and have a quick look that I did and, Lo, there was a massive pile of fish upon my wish. One bin bag full of unopened packets of crisps, one bin bag full of dairy leftovers – yoghurt, soft cheese, milkshakes, etc – most with today's or yesterday's date on them. Well naturally I piled as much as I could into my bag with much fervour and nervousness and then later checked what I'd got. Certainly enough to be able to sleep in my tent by the Danube instead of shoving myself in the way of people who would look after me. I had a princely meal of crisps dipped in some kind of cheese dip and loads of yoghurt and made the first fire I'd made since Richard went home.

The next evening when I was approaching Grein I was overtaken by two jogging men who said something friendly to me in German, so I said, "1. I don't speak German, and 2. Where can I put my tent tonight in Grein?" but I had to start jogging a bit so as not to disturb their rhythm. After a little thought one of them, Archi, said, "Would you like to sleep in a bed instead?" and so we became friends. The next challenge was that I was jogging with my backpack on and if I'd carried on then I would have probably died within about five minutes, so we made a meeting point in town and I couldn't have been happier. Or so I thought.

Just before I got there I noticed a big Aldi or something on the path and I thought maybe I won't be holding Archi up too much if I just quickly pop over and check their bins. And I found another fish upon my wish. Namely, the only thing that had been missing from my life up until then: a kilo of cheese. And with my new haul I arrived at the meeting point at the same time as Archi and he took me out to dinner with the other jogging guy and I put my cheese in his fridge and he almost persuaded me to stay with him for another day but two days off in one month is a little decadent so I contented myself with a massive lounge in the morning. Also, Archi was a conspiracy theorist, with theories of conspiracy about the moon landing, who really started WWII, who organised 9/11, and something about aliens landing in ancient Babylon.

Since then I've found quite a lot of food in bins and have been surviving more off that than hospitality which is quite exciting to start with but certainly more lonely. Luckily for me I met another co-pilgrim: Lucas, who is biking to Tanzania and stopped for a quick chat when he saw my rucksack which turned into him walking with me for the whole day and then camping with me as well. He only had a tarp, which is what cool people call a piece of tarpaulin. No tent. Pretty hardcore, I thought, and he also had other cool things like an espresso maker and an axe which I was quite jealous of. I tried to show him the joys of dumpster diving but everywhere we tried we found nothing. That's what you get for trying to show off.

Another thing that happened which is quite funny is that I slept in a sort of container in the Steckbauers' garden. When I had dropped my stuff there I followed Herr Steckbauer back to his house (a walk of about 30 seconds) and had dinner with them and chatted. When it was time to leave I was mildly concerned that I might not find the container (even though I had instructions and had also walked it before) because my sense of direction isn't very good. Also when I first came through their garden I remember having a small conversation about the pond which, Peter told me, was 3m deep and you could swim in in the summer. My worries proved to be founded when I walked out of their house, down the first 5m of their path and SPLISH into the pond, breaking a thin layer of ice as I did so.

And another thing that happened is that one night the stars came out. I've been thinking about the stars every night for over a month and every night it's cloudy, so I was quite immoderately delighted. And it was warm enough to watch them and check my map and find new constellations and such. I reckon to be able to identify Zwillinge, Fuhrmann, Kleiner Hund and Grosser Hund, Grosser Bar, Cassiopeia and I think Polaris and Castor and Pollux. Which is a big step up from just Orion, but soon I'll know all of them. Now I need a map with pictures of the animals on it because although there are about 20 stars in the Grosser Bar it still doesn't look anything like a bear, but it does look a bit like a scorpion. If that slightly overindulgent paragraph doesn't reflect how much I think about the stars, I should also mention that after about a day in my company, Lucas said, "Whenever I see the stars I'll think about how much you are enjoying them." It occurred to me then that maybe I'd been banging on about them quite a bit.

Bizarrely my own father has requested more information about the lavs here, so if you are of a nervous disposition, skip to the next bit. I suppose anyone except Dad should really skip to the next bit, but then maybe you already have. Well they do of course have those ridiculous shelves which catch your poo ready for inspection. That's a scientific fact which you will believe if you have been to Germany and probably won't if you haven't, but they really do. The drawbacks of this system are:

- it stinks
- the flush is often not powerful enough to sweep the poo away
- there isn't necessarily enough space

and the advantages are:

- you can inspect your own poo.

The only advantage would be considered a disadvantage by most right-minded people, but I come down on the side of the Germans on this one. I think overall it's good that there's a country mental enough to have produced such a thing and obviously good that that country wasn't England.

Anyway, that's enough about lavs, what about my bowels? Well you may not know this but I've had diarrhoea for the last several days and at any given time I might suddenly need to get to a bog within five minutes. And you know the classic Bond-style bomb defusing situation where you've only got five minute and it's all going well and then you cut the wrong wire and suddenly it drops down to five seconds? Well that happens too. And rarely enough so that I let my guard down quite a lot. Naturally this pilgrimage is a particularly good opportunity to play Bowel Roulette because I'm often in situations where it is totally inappropriate to suddenly have to go to the lav –like the time I was staying in someone's house and had just eaten a huge amount of their food (not unconnected, I think) and they were kind of watching me arrange my bed area and their child was using the downstairs loo to have a shower. I got through it with reasonable success but I think I can confidently say that my host family were not unaware of my situation.

This is where you should skip to if you skipped that last bit.

Route

From Passau I've pretty much kept to the Danube bike path, going via: Esternberg, Engelhartszel, Au (the first Au), Feldkirchen, Ottensheim, Au (the second one), Linz, Mitterkirchen, Saxen, Persenbeug (where I felt insanely pleased with myself for going off the bike path for a little while to cut out a curve of the Danube. Later I walked about 3km down a spit which I then walked back, making it 1-1 that day between me and the Danube) and now I'm in Vienna.

Eastern Europe

March 24, 2009

Slovakians and Hungarians

For a while now I've been thinking it would be nice to get out of German speaking territory and into somewhere new. I hope that doesn't sound a bit mean but traditionally when you visit a country you just go for a week or something and I'd been there for ages. Long enough to learn German almost perfectly.

But then, when I got to the edge of Austria there was this massive city made of white tower blocks gleaming away at me on the other side of the river and it all looked a bit unnerving. Every single place I've been to so far looks kind of the same with a little church spire poking out of a bunch of multi-coloured pastel houses, and this place looked totally different. I think it was Bratislava. It managed to shine even through the load of gloom which seems to permanently hover over the Danube.

I carried on walking and then found that I'd accidentally walked into Slovakia (were you expecting that? I wasn't) and then I walked some more and found I'd accidentally walked through Bratislava and out the other side passing precisely one open café to let me know it was a capital city. Then I met some people who apparently didn't speak any English or German who I had a conversation with. They did a lot of acting and gesticulating which I understood precisely none of. I did a bit of acting which they also didn't understand, and then they gave me some biscuits which I did understand. Later I met a guy called Erik when I was putting up my tent and he invited me back to his house to sleep there instead and the next day he came with me. We walked for a few kilometres and were in Hungary. So I've picked up a co-pilgrim in every country, including Slovakia. And that's what the Slovakians are like.

When I sat down for a rest in a pub in Hungary they gave me some soup and then another course (potatoes, rice and some sort of schnitzel – the food is getting stranger for sure) and then yesterday when I sat down in another pub they gave me beer and Jágermeister and when I said that I hoped to be in Gyor tomorrow and Budapest in a week and then Serbia in a month they laughed and shook their heads and said, "Gyor in a week, Budapest in a month, Serbia in three months," and I suppose I saw the logic in that so I stayed there the night in the basement of the pub.

Thank you

Here are a list of ways to say thank you in order of stupidness (starting with the least stupid):

- Thank you
- Danku (Dutch)
- Danke (German)
- Gracias (Spanish)
- Merci (French – this is quite sensible because it's a variant of Mercy, which isn't really to do with thanks, but it's in the broad category of words to do with nice things)

- Chekui (Czech, I think. Well it's something like Cheeky)
- Checkuem (Slovakian and I'm reasonably sure it's not spelt like that, kind of sounds a bit like Requiem which is totally inappropriate)
- Multsumesc (Romanian and could be argued deserves a higher place because it sounds like Lots of Mesc, which might well be something you give someone as a thank you present)
- Kusumu (Hungarian. I have to remember that it's a cross between Cosovo and Wassaname, which takes ages and is stupid).

Hungary (most of)

April 3, 2009

Route

I reckon it's been about two weeks since I was in Vienna and you'll be glad to know that that has been enough time to pretty much cross Hungary. It's totally flat and there are roads everywhere which all go in the right direction for some reason. I'm going to go to Romania next, and then sort of head down to the Danube and then into Bulgaria at some point. I'm not going to go to Serbia any more; they have a totally different alphabet.

Man Cannot Live on Beer Alone…

I suppose the last few weeks have been the best weather for walking that I'm likely to see, and they weren't wonderful. When I arrived in Hungary I had the impression that it was a pretty hostile place. There was a mental wind buffeting me around and even though it was behind me most of the time I pretty much wished it would go away. That Irish guy who said, "May the wind always be at your back," probably meant to also say, "If there's got to be a wind at all." Or, "But only a nice gentle breeze." Weirdly it's much worse than rain or cold, which is probably why Bunyan was talking about, "Come wind come weather." At first I thought he just put it in because it scanned but I get it now. When I said to people, "Is it always this windy?" they just said, "It's Hungary!" and other non-encouraging things like that. And then I ran out of food and began to be a bit hungry and I thought, Oh Dear. But that's just an illustration of how much of a big idiot I am and that I never learn. Of course I was wrong about the Oh Dear thing – completely wrong.

I mentioned before how the Germanic attitude to me coming into their pub and sitting down and not buying anything was often to give me a meal or at least a coffee. The Hungarian attitude is similar but different, in that either the manager or, more often, one of the scattering of old men in overalls (not the one pumping money into the fruit machine, one of the others) buys me a beer. Then I explain through mime and by reading the phrases on my piece of soggy A4 which I keep in my pocket that I'm going to Jerusalem and then someone else buys me more beer and sometimes – eugh – palinka. That's a kind of vodka which is normally homemade but which they confusingly translate as "Schnaps." And when I ask them if it's schnaps or palinka they get very excited and say, "Aha! Palinka!" because I know the name so I must like it.

My sister Millie once told me that alcohol is the fifth food group and sits somewhere between carbohydrate and fat in terms of energy content per gram, so I try to always accept booze when I'm thinking about my survival. But a wiser fella than myself once said, "Man cannot live on beer alone, but sausage and the occasional slice of bread is also quite useful." Luckily for me the Hungarian's are most generous with all three. After Győr I walked to Pannonhalma where I was given a two course meal in a restaurant, a couple of slices of bread for my bag, and two massive oily sausage type things – the kind that don't need cooking and that mould doesn't want to eat. In the evening I reached Táp and asked some guy in my best Hungarian (pointing and mime) if I could put my tent up somewhere. He started phoning people and told me to wait, so I waited. He then bought me a Hungarian speciality, cow's stomach and pig's trotter stew. I was given quite a lot of it and although it tasted nice I have to admit I was grossed out a bit. I finished it, but I didn't ask for seconds. A little later Emma turned up in her car and spoke English and I stayed at their house (her husband is called Attila, which is a name that seems to have gone out of fashion in England) and in the morning she gave me a massive tube of paté, a loaf of bread and a couple of sausages. Since then I haven't run out of sausage and at the time of writing I have three and a half sausages (as well as 6 hard boiled eggs) in my bag.

The other day I was out of bread – I had lots of meat but nothing to go with it – and someone was busy buying me beer so I said, "Actually I'd slightly prefer bread," and since there wasn't any in the bar he bought me some crisps. But another guy, hearing the news that I was short of bread, nipped next door and came back with a massive hunk of "bacon," a sausage, a large jar of jam and two slices of bread. That's the sort of attitude they have to bread round here. And the reason I say '"bacon"' rather than just 'bacon' is that this is that stuff I was given before in Austria with no red bit in it, you just cut off hunks of fat and eat that with bread, and if you have a microwave you can microwave it and then dip your bread in what's left. It's delicious; I don't know why we don't do it in England. Everyone does it here, even girls. It's totally normal. And it makes perfect sense because fat tastes nice.

Gypsies

Apart from all that sausage talk, I should mention the Gypsies. When I was a little bit lost and still walking uncharacteristically late I blundered into a group of park rangers and bird ringers who were having a party with much palinka and I was ushered in and given a bed (as well as some palinka, natch). In the morning they said, "Don't stop in Hantos, there are lots of Gypsies there." Later that day someone else said, "When you get to Sárosd, keep going, it's a bad place," and he did mimes which indicated that I would probably die if I stopped there and I got the impression that it was Gypsy related. I've never been one to take other people's prejudices too seriously so when I got to Sárosd I sat down for a moment in the first bar I got to. In general I'm quite good at putting up with a bit of a ramshackle atmosphere and I'd even say I prefer a slightly scruffy place to an overly sophisticated one but there are certain things which anyone would hope for as a kind of minimum comfort requirement. Like, for instance, it should really have paper in the lav and you'd like to be sure that the glasses get cleaned between use and such. I think you could also say that you would always want to be (to the nearest percent) 100% sure that no children would try to prostitute their grandmother to you, and in this bar I was about 60% sure that I was being propositioned in this way by a nine-year-old boy. I said, "Nem irtem" (which means, "I don't understand") again and again until I felt worryingly close to understanding too much and then I made my excuses and left.

The next bar in the same village didn't have a lav at all. They said there was another bar 1km away that did. I held on. So that was Sarósd, a town I'm not in a desperate hurry to revisit. However when I reached Hantos I had recovered my composure a little. It was late enough to stop for the night, so I identified a house which didn't look like it was inhabited by weirdos and I buzzed their buzzer. Someone with a gammy leg and arm hobbled out to meet me and stared at me as I pointed at my tent and did some miming. It occurred to me to wonder whether it was a good sign or a bad sign that he had a physical deformity, but I've watched Deliverance and I've watched Wrong Turn and I knew the answer. No, it was not a good sign. People with physical deformities cannot be trusted. He barked something or other and then went back inside and a bit later his wife came out. Well it turned out that they were delightful people who cleared some space in their spare room for me to sleep in and gave me dinner and then breakfast in the morning. When I left the deformed barky guy gave me an affectionate pat on the arm to let me know that I should have been thinking about The BFG, not Deliverance.

Inappropriate Gifts

I mentioned the jam, didn't I? Totally inappropriate, way too heavy. But not, by some distance, the most inappropriately heavy. Here they are, in descending order:

1. Half a turkey. After I had eaten it (there was tons) I realised how much of it was bone (tons).
2. Pot of jam
3. (I reloaded the jam with sugar in a restaurant, and someone saw me doing this and came back with) Two more pots of jam
4. Two litres of orangeade (although this wasn't too bad because I drank it as I walked)
5. Two bottles of homemade wine, one red, one Chardonnay. Particularly inappropriate because they were decanted not into plastic bottles nor even into wine bottles, but into liqueur bottles which are super heavy. I was slightly sad not to be hit by a car and hospitalised when I had the wine because I'm sure it would have made me look cool.

Weather

It did stop being windy. The next day it was clear it was just a lie about Hungary being windy. It has also stopped being cold. For the last two days it has been like English summer at its height, in that I have got burnt while walking and have generally been thinking a lot about wearing shorts and jettisoning my extra jumper and hat. I'm already thinking about rearranging my sleeping schedule to incorporate a siesta and I've got a feeling that I'm going to slow down a bit from now on.

Kit

My stick seems to have developed what, in the world of conkering, is known as a death crack. Well I think it's a death crack but it has been there without developing for a few weeks so maybe it's just a crack. There's not much I can do about it so I'm just going to wait and see, but I'm against reinforcing it with metal or something because then it'll become a piece of technology instead of a stick and goodness knows I don't need any more technology.

I have worn my therma-wicking-mohair-composite-ultralite every day and almost every night since I left and I have just noticed a small hole has developed under my rucksack strap. Apart from that it's still wicking as new.

My boots are still in good order. Due to slightly conflicting foot/shoe shapes my big toe on my left foot is never totally comfortable, but on the plus side it gives rise to some really gross photos.

My socks, which I think are more remarkable than the boots since they're only made of wool, are still unblemished since I was given them in Adelsheim (1000km behind me). I told Frau Pittner that I strongly doubted they would make it to Jerusalem, but now I'm not so sure.

My mattress, which at first was such a blessing is now starting to take on the shape and weight of ballast. Hopefully I'll offload it on Abi if she ever turns up.

Three Cooked Meals

Have you ever had three cooked meals in one day? I have, when I was at school. We used to have three every day. But since then it has become something of a rarity. I think the first time this trip was in Hungary when I had a breakfast of bread and sausage (not cooked), then goulash cooked on a fire in the garden in a dangling pot (Hungarian version of a barbeque, cooked by the man of the house), then when I sat down in a restaurant I was quickly presented with a Cuban burger thing and for supper I had a massive load of chilli at the rangers' party. I'm living in the lap of luxury.

Dogs

If you ever walk through a Hungarian village you'll probably notice that there are a billion dogs everywhere. And they're almost all either vicious or bored, which means that an opportunity to bark at someone (me) is never unwelcome. One game to play with them is to psyche up the first dog in the street and then walk along and watch as all the other dogs join in the frenzy one by one. I call that one Dogmino Rally. A variant is to try to sneak through an entire village without setting off the Mexican Woof (which is much easier if it's raining).

IBS

I'm imagining the bit about my bowels is probably the most interesting thing I've written so far, so I think I'll write something about my new medical complaint, which I haven't heard of before but I presume would probably be called Irritable Bladder Syndrome: for some reason my bladder, which used to work reasonably well, has shrivelled to about the capacity of a plastic cup (though I haven't measured yet). I rarely sleep through an entire night without weeing and the other day I went three times as well as in the morning. Now what on earth has happened there? Not enough salt? Too much salt? Some non-salt related reason?

Summary

Hungarians are cool. There seems to be no inappropriate time for a quick glass of wine. I'm eating enough. I'm probably going to start burning soon. There are dogs everywhere. Romania next. I need a wee.

Getting to Romania

April 11, 2009

Police

One of the things I wanted to do on this pilgrimage was to get kicked out of a country by the police. Well I've done that now. I was ejected from Romania by the very efficient border control who spotted my illegal entry and diverted me. I thought I'd head across the Hungary/Romania border from Kubekhasa to Beba Veche since there were nice small roads and although there wasn't a little sign on the map saying that there was a legitimate crossing and although lots of people told me I wouldn't be able to cross there, I knew that Romania was part of the EU these days so I'd be ok.

When I got there the last person I spoke to about it drew a very careful map of how to go back the way I'd come and then did a good impression of soldiers killing me which was meant to warn me not to try to cross the border through the fields. But he did point the direction of the border and I said I'd go and have a look. There was no sign of soldiers or killing so I tentatively stepped forward. Then it became obvious that I could easily just walk to Beba Veche, which I could see, and that no one would stop me.

When I arrived there a policeman ambled up to me, looked at my passport, took me to the station and we did a lot of waiting. I had been spotted. They called the Hungarian border patrol who drove up to the border several hours later, then drove away to be replaced by another Hungarian border patrol, this time with Romanian translator, who took me to Cenad in a car. Well actually in three different cars. The whole process took several hours and several people and when I was dropped in Cenad, which is a border which you are allowed to walk through, I walked through with no problems. Now I'm legal, and it's almost exactly as it would have been if I had walked across to Beba Veche without being spotted, only I moved 20km east in a car, so that's the end of Pilgrimage 1. Pilgrimage 2 started in Cenad and hopefully I'll get to Jerusalem this time. Also, I got a fine for 15,000 Forint (£47) which I have to pay in 30 days. Goodness knows how I'm going to do that.

Gypsies Again

Another thing I wanted to do was to be robbed by Gypsies and luckily I was able to strike this off my list as well on my first day in Romania. As I walked into Cenad a friendly looking character was sitting outside his house and waved me over. I said I was looking for a place to put my tent up and he pointed at his garden and I thought, "Cool, I've made a friend already," and then he made me coffee and so I was right. Then he said, "Are you hungry?" and I had just learnt how to say, "I'm always hungry," in Romanian so I proudly stuttered my way through that and he told me that there was a shop in town and that he'd take me if I liked. Well that wasn't the right answer, he was meant to say, "Here, have some food," and then I told him I had no money and he still didn't say, "Here, have some food." That made me smell a rat, especially because he asked a few questions about whether I really did have no money (actually I had thirty Euros, but I always say I have no money because I was planning on giving it away and it's too complicated to explain all that). A bit later he invited me into his house to watch TV and I said, yes OK, and at the same time his friend turned up who didn't look at me when he shook my hand and was a bit squinty and suspicious looking. I sort of had the feeling that he might be there to look through my stuff, so when I went to bed a bit later I checked my stuff and I had no Euros any more. Everything else was where it had been so either he knew where I kept it somehow (in my compass – too obvious?) or he was an effective sneakthief. Either way I slept unsoundly that night, thinking that maybe some other sting would be effected on me to get anything else I might be hoarding. Particularly since after I had gone to sleep Squinter knocked on my tent and tried to make me come and eat some food. He was reasonably forceful and as a result I turned down the offer of a meal with more vigour than I have in months. Unnervingly he also shoved his head into my tent and looked around, without explanation. In the morning he was back and because really they'd not done anything wrong and also (mostly) because I wanted to lose a bit of weight from my bag, I gave Alin my jumper as a no-hard-feelings present. Then I shook hands and didn't mention my money and scuttled out of there like a massive chicken.

One small downside to this incident is that the church in Jerusalem which was meant to get twenty Euros won't get it. A bigger downside is that I have become a practicing racist since then. I have been reliably told that there are nice Gypsies around so I have an open mind, but since my only experiences so far have been a bit negative, I am in the ugly position of judging people by their ethnicity. Hopefully I'll meet some of the good type soon.

An hour after leaving Alin, in case this seems a little gloom heavy, I was given breakfast and 10 Lei (£2) by someone, then later a sausage or two by someone else, another meal a bit later, and in the evening an omelette (four eggs) with sausages followed by an omelette (two eggs) by some other people. Poor old Alin. All he needs to do is wander around with a stick and instead he steals off his friends.

A Week or Two of Romania

April 16, 2009

What Romanians Are Like

You may be wondering what Romanians are like and so far I've only mentioned the Gypsies. I think it's only fair to separate them because so far they've behaved quite differently. When I arrived in Romania and got scammed a little bit, it unnerved me somewhat and put me a bit on the defensive. Since then I've met a few other Gypsies and they've ranged from being friendly but in a sort of only-because-I'm-about-to-ask-you-for-money way to unpleasantly hounding and I still have an overall negative view of them. I didn't think that would happen to me and I'm still waiting for the time when I meet the nice ones. I'm sure they're around.

Romanians, however, (the non-Gypsy ones) are like this: the border police, while busting me (which took ages), gave me a massive meal. The owners of a grocery store slash brothel gave me two massive sausages and some tinned meat. A roaringly drunk guy fried some eggs for me which I ate sitting among the hens that laid them and the pub slash grocery store where I found him gave me a loaf of bread to eat it with. A family of quite brown people (they weren't Gypsies; I asked) gave me an omelette with sausages followed by another omelette and since it isn't really veggie season, pretty much all of these meals have been accompanied by gherkins. Another guy brought me a polystyrene tray with chicken and eggs for supper when I'd put my tent up. Two people who worked in a motel gave me a whole load of meat and such. A farmer who I met quite late, maybe at 9, when I was thoroughly exhausted from having just managed to shake off a Gypsy scamster (which involved him following me for ages and yabbering about how I should buy his mobile for five Euros), didn't say anything but just nodded that I could sleep in his field and then in the morning he gave me some hard boiled eggs and a hunk of cooked meat (cooked, not smoked, and at least half of it was flesh and not fat so it tasted a bit unusual).

Another character bought me a beer and a coffee and then called the police who duly turned up and checked my passport. That was a bit weird, but I think in Romania although the levels of goodness and generosity are as high as anywhere else (actually I think higher than Western Europe – I have been eating three or four meals every day and am normally in a rush to finish whatever is in my bag so it won't go bad), the levels of distrust are higher too. Whereas a French person would hear that I have no money and I'm walking to Jerusalem and think, "Oh! Mon Dieu! Those crazy English," and a German person would think, "But have you got enough maps and the appropriate footwear?" and a Hungarian would say "Jerusalem? By foot? Haha! You drink palinka? Get him a palinka!" a Romanian is more inclined to think, "Is this guy some kind of illegal scamster?"

Another thing that Romanians are like is that they don't all go to the pub to drink all day like the Hungarians do. In fact, in any given village there may not even be a pub, but instead they have grocery store slash cafés called "Magasin Mixt" where you can sit outside and drink if you like, but mostly people don't. Instead the idle just loiter around on the street outside their houses waiting for something interesting to happen, and wherever I go I am that interesting thing. When I get to a place the timid eyeball me from where they are and the bold come up to me and say, "Where are you going?" and when they find that I'm English they summon the town polyglot who will find out in either German or French or, if I'm lucky, English what I'm up to and relay it to everyone else. This process often gathers a crowd, particularly of children, who are almost always very comfortable staring at me. Luckily I'm quite comfortable being stared at because otherwise I would have been a bit put off my food on certain occasions.

Also Romanians are quite fond of growing their own stuff instead of buying it from Tesco, a trait they share with Hungarians. That means I normally get given stuff which is homemade – which also means that I get a large amount of whatever's in season (eggs at the moment, and "cheese" or "Mozarella" as one imaginative person called it). Less and less people say, "This is made here," as it seems to be less a matter of pride and more just the way things are done.

Church

There are two Easters in Romania, one on Easter and one a week later. The Orthodox church for some reason celebrate it later and on Easter they have something called Florin Sunday which is like the Saint's Day of people who have flowers' names. Can you imagine? I met a couple of people called Florin to prove that it wasn't a total waste of time. Also they have a weird system where you get Easter Monday off, but only your Easter Monday, so when you sign up for a job you have to say whether you are Orthodox or not so they know when to give you a day off. I think that's true, but I'm not totally sure – it seems so unlikely. On the real Easter I woke up in a town with only an Orthodox church so after I'd eaten my fried eggs and bacon (brought to my tent by two boys who crouched down and watched me eat it) I went to church.

It's a funny old affair. When anyone comes in the first thing to do is go up to a table which has some things on it – an engraving and a couple of pictures or something – and kiss certain parts of them. Everyone except me did this: I didn't realise I was meant to until it was too late. Then you go and shake hands with the people on your row and then, if you feel like it, you can buy a candle or five from the candle seller who is right in the middle. If you've bought a candle you can then leave for a bit, presumably to light your candle somewhere, though I didn't find out where, then you come back and settle down. Since there isn't really a start time, you just do all this as the service is going on. And the service, at least the bit I went to, involved an old woman singing for a bit until the priest turned up and got dressed into his finery. Then the priest took over the main brunt of the singing, occasionally stopping to let the old woman do a response (and she had been joined by some old men by then). Every so often he would say a keyword and everyone would stand up for a bit or do a cross or something. I think if you stay for the whole lot you get three and a half hours and at the end there's a sermon, but I only stayed for an hour or so. When I left the watchers from breakfast were still there, waiting for me.

In the evening I walked past a church which seemed like there might be some action and it turned out that they were about to have a service and that they were Pentecostal. That was a stroke of thoroughly good fortune. Before the vicar took the reins one of the old women of the congregation, instead of just sitting there, would shout out a number and everyone sang it. There wasn't any accompaniment and nor was there any need because unlike almost every other church in the world (by which I mean the ones I've been to in England), the people seemed to like singing. And I liked the music. It was sort of rhythmic and folky and one of the women had the sort of croaky semi-real voice that only exist on archive films from a hundred years ago. Though that doesn't explain it very well so I'll say this instead – it was extraordinary and beautiful. There were three solos during the service and a poetry reading and despite – not despite, because of – all that, I thought it was an excellent service. When it finished, the entire congregation moved towards the door, blocking it, then turned towards me and did some high quality staring. I mumbled, "Nu vorbesc Romanesc Eu sunt Englese" at no one in particular, which gave everyone something to talk about and softened the stare. An Anglophone was found and pushed forward and a few moments later I was eating chicken and fried mashed potato and if you'd like to know how to make mashed potato better, it's simple: fry them.

Smell

I also went to a reformed church where afterwards the minister told me to come with him to his house and I was the recipient of a bed for the first time in ages. That was wonderful but it made me notice a new development which has come with the hot weather (did I mention that it's hot here? It is). Every evening I am made aware of the smell (strong and unpleasant) of my feet and every morning I clamp them up in my boots and forget about it for the day. However when I was the guest of Francisc and Dora I was thrown into a quandary. It was obvious to me that I should walk round their house in my boots and not in my socks, but it was hard to explain why. I chose the direct approach, doing impressions of an unpleasant odour and asking if I could wash my feet. Well I took my heinous socks off which had acquired a good deal of sock butter (hardens overnight and melts almost immediately when I put the sock on again giving the feeling of walking on a slice of raw bacon), washed my feet in the bath and put on some clean(ish) socks but it was already too late. There were black marks on the rug where I had trodden with my bare foot and what was undeniably a stench in the air. No one said anything but when I went back later the window and door were open and later still Francisc offered me a sanitary pack of soap, toothpaste, toothbrush and socks.

Jam

I can't believe how rude I was about being given jam. Since then I've had a maximum of four pots of jam on me and a minimum (yesterday) of half. I love it. For a while now I have not been hungry at all. Not even in my mind. For a decent stretch of this walk I have had the mind of a starving man, constantly thinking of food and how I was going to find it. In my sensible moments I knew there was no point in thinking like this but there it is. One of my most constant fantasies was of finding a bag of Starbucks muffins, the like of which I used to throw away every day when I worked there (for the super-interested, I think they've now changed the shelf life of muffins from one day to two days which should mean a significant drop in muffin waste) and which I used to take home and pick little bits off before throwing away in my bin. At times on this walk I wouldn't have picked little bits off, I would have cheerfully eaten a sackful. Now, however, and especially with the advent of jam, I seem to have enough sugar in my life. Enough sugar and enough everything else.

Indiana Mikey

Two days ago I took a shortcut through the Cheile Nerei-Beuşniţa national park and only halfway through I got to an impassable bit. The map doesn't show it but there's a drop of twenty feet or so which you need a rope for, so I diverted my path up a dry river bed which was flanked by trees marked with a red stripe. Obviously it was a different path and so it would lead somewhere. Much later still the dry river bed I was walking up started to get wet and to stop being so much a river bed and more of a river. And it got dark. I climbed the hill to find a place for my tent, found quite a good place and noticed a red mark on one of the trees. In a matter of minutes I worked out that the red marks which I had been following were everywhere in the park. So I wasn't so much following a path as just walking into a river. After sleeping, and waking up, and eating breakfast, and traversing many dangerous obstacles, etc, I was back at a road. To celebrate, I ate a whole pot of jam. Eating jam from the pot should be really good but I still felt a bit guilty that I wasn't diluting it with bread.

A few times I've been running low on food and sort of economised, like by not eating jam straight from the pot, and then later I've been given tons of jam or whatever and I've thought, "Idiot! Why did I save my jam when I was hungry?" Now my motto is: "When I'm hungry, eat my food." Also, once someone gave me some delicious turkey which made my mouth water and two days later it had gone mouldy and I cut bits off and threw them away. I still feel bad about that; now my plan is never to get into that sort of situation again. Much better to risk having no food for a little bit, especially since it never actually happens.

Hungarian Fine

Don't worry about that, it's fine. It's Hungary that wants it and I'm not in Hungary any more. I think it says something about how if I don't pay then they'll do such and such and if

I'm not an EU member then I may get banned from Hungary. Well I don't want that any more than you do, so I'll probably get round to sorting it out at some point.

Gypsies and Racists in Romania

April 23, 2009

Gypsies

Aha! We all knew it was coming and here it is – nice Gypsies! One of the things that Gypsies like to do is tell you after not very long that they're Gypsies so although I can't tell by looking at them I'm reasonably good at knowing if someone's a Gypsy or not. One such group who were loitering around outside a Magasin Mixt drinking beer started talking to me. After a while one of them bought me a beer so I could loiter as efficiently as them and then a little later one of them suggested that maybe I was in need of female company but in quite a discrete way which wasn't really very alarming. Then, just as I was bracing myself for whatever shakedown they had in mind, they all left. I finished my beer by myself and thought, "Well, that does it, Gypsies are nice after all." In the evening I walked past someone's house and a little boy was there and he delightedly darted inside to tell everyone to come out and look at the English person. As soon as his aunt saw me she said, "You want some food? A coffee?" and because I am a suspicious type of person I didn't immediately say, "Yes Please," because I was thinking, "This feels like some sort of Gypsy trap." Then I remembered the lesson I'd learnt earlier and so I changed my mind. With much speed and enthusiasm I was given a plate of eggs and bacon and other stuff that had been imported from Austria and a French-speaking person was unearthed from the family and I was persuaded to stay the night. Furthermore they were Orthodox and it was Holy Saturday for them and they have a midnight mass for Easter as well as Christmas which I wouldn't have gone to otherwise. Even furthermore they have a massive Easter Sunday meal with every conceivable animal cooked in some Romanian way and a whole load of cakes and such which I also joined in with. They taught me how to do the sign of the cross properly (two fingers together with a thumb and it goes head, stomach, right shoulder, left shoulder – I'd been doing any old thing) and they gave me loads of food to take with me (to add to my already loads of food) including boiled Easter eggs, which are painted red for the blood of Christ. After midnight mass there are bonfires on the streets around town which people sit round and drink and dance and we went to a Gypsy one but by then I was a little too shattered to enjoy it. The mother of the family had been a Baptist when she'd married and unable to have children; four years later she converted to Orthodoxism and since then has had seven children so that just goes to show you.

Racists

So I'm still a racist but less than I was before. But while we're on the subject: I also met a couple of racists who were very nice to me. They'd bought a bunch of land which they were working on when I walked past and they welcomed me over and spoke excellent English. After a while the woman (who was German) said, "Are there many auslanders where you live?" and I said words to the effect of, "No, hardly any," and before I'd finished my sentence she said, "Gut, gut. I am little bit racist. I don't like all this niggers come to England and Germany. It's not Africa. It's England." I didn't quite know what to say to that but I said that I quite liked living in East London because there were lots of curry houses. She didn't like foreign food either, so that wasn't an excuse for her. When we weren't talking about race, which came up every so often (Me: Fort Lauderdale is a funny place. Her: Yes, it's nice, but too many Spics) they seemed to be the type of people I quite like in that they were funny and friendly and interesting and one of them was called Elvis and other things. So now I've had to modify my view of both Gypsies and racists. Well I don't have much else to do.

More Romania

April 28, 2009

Romanian Life

When I got to Romania I wrote in my little book, "Things I've seen: A donkey pulling a cart with two women in it; an old man in a trilby winching water from a well; a horse and a goat wandering around on the street; a pub lav being a hole in the floor," but that was only after a day or two. These days none of those things have any effect on me because they're all so commonplace. Running water here isn't unusual but it isn't the norm either. Most villages have a few communal wells and a lot of private wells in people's gardens and it's standard practice to winch your water. I'd never used a well before I got here and now I do it quite often.

Horse and cart, also, are standard methods of transport. In one town, Timişoara I think, where there was a busy and fast dual carriageway, I saw a horse pulling a family in a cart turn into the road in the wrong direction, get overtaken by a few people and then dart across to the other side. It looked frantically dangerous but only raised a few beeps from the oncoming motorists. Donkey and cart and cow and cart are less common but still not unusual. And the things they tow around are always a bit surprising. Things like a bundle of really long sticks and a Dacia's exhaust pipe, or a three piece suite. With generally more than 2 people balanced on there as well.

The running water situation means that most people have an outhouse which turns out to be not particularly unpleasant. I suppose the unpleasant bit is when you clean them out, which I haven't yet got involved with, but to use, it's no big problem. Nor is the great outdoors and now I'm armed with my own bogroll I've been taking advantage of Mother Earth's facilities as well, which is slightly better because you get to have a small bonfire afterwards which is quite satisfying.

Thusly I've been keeping the diarrhoea at bay with no hugely embarrassing poo-related stories as a result.

IBS

Relatedly, here's a full update on my bodily functions: my bladder problem is restricted to precisely one symptom – tiny bladder. It's as if it has shrunk. I wee about twice a night depending on how much I've drunk. At first I quite devoutly followed Mum's suggestion that I drink lots (LOTS) of water (WATER) but then I noticed that it was because she thought I was dehydrated. Well I know what dehydrated means: it means thirsty. And the symptoms are not that your bladder shrinks to half its normal size, but that you want a drink and your wee is yellow. And I'm not dehydrated because I don't want a drink and my wee is normal colour.

The other suggestion was that I have some sort of bacterial infection which suited me quite well because Dr Wallace told us in Biology that we have white blood cells which identify the bacteria and then sort of smother them and kill them and remember what they looked like so I can't ever be infected again. So basically all I had to do was wait for a bit and I'd fix myself, but I've waited and it's not better. Still, no big deal, it's just a matter of weeing more often and it's not like I'm particularly pushed for time at the moment.

Feet

Though I haven't really washed very much recently (related to the running water issue previously discussed), when I do get the opportunity I'm caught on the horns of a small dilemma. At the moment my feet don't hurt when I walk, partly due to a decently callused foot. But when I wash my feet the callus bit goes soft and white and then comes off. If I cunningly wash them quickly so the calluses don't have time to go soft and white, they stay smelly. The smelly bit turns out to be the useful bit. So basically my feet stink, but I'm just going to carry on using the same defence I've always used – hiding them in my boots.

Food

Did I ever say about my hunger? Well I was hungry before, in the German speaking countries, and now I'm not. In fact, back in the German speaking countries I weighed myself anxiously a couple of times and converted the numbers I saw into stone to see whether or not I should be worried about it. I think I weighed 76kg. For the last few weeks I've had such a glut of food in my bag, lots of which was fresh, that I've struggled to eat it all before it went bad.

Rory's suggestion that maybe talking to people in a hopeful and hungry way was, in fact, just a form of begging seemed to me to imply that what he thought I really should do is to hide from anyone who might give me food as much as I can. Recently I have been doing that, not because I don't want to seem like a beggar but because if I talk to anyone for any length of time they foist food on me. Hundreds of food! Tons of it. So I try to sneak through the towns on my route without being noticed – with limited success. I haven't had the chance to weigh myself recently but I have again that reassuring grabbable slice of fat around my stomach. In Easter week, for example, I think I ate a minimum of four hard boiled eggs on any day and I reckon an average of five or so. Maybe even more. That's a high daily average even for an egg enthusiast.

Easter

Before Easter everyone (actually everyone's mother) makes about a thousand hard boiled eggs and colours them red somehow. Then, when Easter comes, you get one of the eggs and someone else gets another one and you say, "Christ is risen," and they say, "He is risen indeed," and then you tap your eggs together until one of them breaks. The person whose egg breaks is the loser and then you eat your egg. Those are the standard rules of the red egg game, but there's another variant where you see a stranger walking through your town and you just give him red eggs. Two old men who were talking to each other hailed me down to hear my story and afterwards one of them produced, from his pocket I think, though it wasn't obvious, a red egg and gave it to me. A guy in a car who stopped to ask if I wanted a lift gave me a red egg. I have a container which fits a maximum of 10 and still I often had to turn down egg offers. Last Sunday I was given a red egg and two normal eggs for lunch so I think it's the end of the red egg season. But it was excellent while it lasted.

Romanian Towns

When I walk through a town in Romania this is what happens: everyone stares at me, always. I always nod at people and say, "Buna Zeua," and smile and sometimes even that doesn't stop the staring. Quite small towns are often laid out along one road, so they last for quite a while and after a bit of walking someone usually asks me where I'm going or where I'm from and I still often get it wrong. And some people, instead of asking, just flick their chin up and wibble their hand and that's it. Then they stare at me some more. I still don't know how to respond to this. Normally I say, "Eo sunt Englaise" and that seems to do the trick. It isn't a hostile gesture though, as I found out when one guy did it and then asked me if I wanted any food. I said, "No," since I'd just eaten and had a bag full, and then he offered me coffee and I said, "Yes." And then his parents gave me a massive meal and some red eggs regardless of my claims.

When I have been accosted successfully a bunch of people gather round and ask me questions in Romanian and when I don't understand (which is most of the time) they just ask me again but louder, or sometimes one of the other people asks me again and eventually I explain enough for them to either fetch a person who speaks French or give me food or leave me alone. Then I walk further into the town and the whole thing happens again, sometimes just 100m away, in sight of the first batch of people. If I'm lucky I acquire a follower who answers all the preliminary questions for me.

Police

Last night a new and slightly ridiculous development took place. I had set up my tent underneath a massive electricity pylon which I thought was quite funny and as I was eating my sandwich and drinking my beer the police turned up and told me I wasn't allowed to stay there. Not because I was breaking any particular law but because there were lots of "banditos" around and, worse still, Gypsies. After a lot of pleading they let me stay there but wrote down everything in my passport (pretty much every police station in Romania now has my full details) and alerted the nearby petrol station and found out my route.

It seemed that there was no real harm in telling him my route but when I arrived in Drănic I was met by a policeman who had been instructed to guard me and make sure I got to wherever I was going. Now it seems I am to have a relay escort of police taking me through from town to town. I'm sure the Gypsy armies who are after me won't have a chance now.

Pigs

If you want to wake someone up you could do a lot worse than killing a pig near them. I walked over to see what all the squealing was about and found that the trotters were already off and they were getting to work on the head.

The End of Romania and the Beginning of Bulgaria

May 5, 2009

Abi

My friend Abi came to visit me the other day and totally ruined all my plans. For some reason she wasn't able to just come and find me by telling the taxi driver to drive along my route and stop when she saw me. Instead I had to not just divert from my original course, but change countries completely. I'd planned to spend as little time in Bulgaria as I could because they have a totally different alphabet but since Abi's flight went to Bulgaria and she was being lame I had to go and meet her there. I was a little bit anxious because I couldn't afford the ferry having spent my last three Euros (10 Lei) handing out cake that morning to people in the street (delightfully, pretty much everyone took one without any questioning and mostly didn't say thank you or anything, which I suppose is the other side of being a really generous country, generosity isn't particularly surprising to them). So I anxiously walked past the long line of lorries to the ticket person and said, when she asked my name, "Um, Mikey Lear, but...I don't have any money..." and she looked up and said, "No money? Ok, go on. It's a present." And that is the story of how I overcame a problem that has been on my mind for about a month.

Then on the other side of the Danube I discovered that I didn't understand anything again. Even a sign which says something like "Internet" looked like "интернет." That's not very useful. Furthermore, no one spoke English and in the bus station, after hopefully listing Engleski, Frenski, Germanski (which felt a lot like I was making fun of them), I tried Romanski and someone else who spoke a little bit of Romanian was brought over to translate. I think what they told me is that Abi's bus would get in at 7.30 just over there, both of which were untrue as it turned out. Another thing I discovered was that Bulgarians, hilariously and (I think) uniquely, have inverted nodding. I mean to say that they nod when they mean "No" and they shake their heads when they mean "Yes." As if a different language base and alphabet isn't enough to contend with. The plus side is that Bulgarians often look pretty funny. Try to imagine what you would look like if you were thoughtfully listening to someone and nodding agreement and then do the same face and everything but change it to a shake instead. You'll find that you've gone from intelligent listener to bewildered simpleton who is hearing something totally beyond his comprehension. Heh heh.

Which all means that Abi turned up somewhere else and an hour later than predicted and we accidentally saw each other while I was being led to an internet café to check my emails and then we hightailed it out of there to a delightful campsite slash petrol station and exchanged presents. She'd got me a Lion bar and I'd got her two litres of homemade red wine (which I was told was called Bear's Blood) and a litre of tsuika. Tsuika is Romanian for palinka and translates as brandy or vodka or whiskey by people who are very keen to translate it into something. It's strong.

Pooscapes

Back to Romania briefly. There are exactly two things I don't like about Romania. I've hinted at the first one before but to make it more explicit, there is an internal racial conflict between the Gypsies and the Romanians. Lots of very nice educated and liberal thinking types really believe that Gypsies are inherently bad people. The police habitually warn me about them and the danger of visiting a village is commonly summed up by, "There are lots of Gypsies there." I suspect that being a Gypsy in that kind of environment brings out their worst qualities though I'm certainly no sociologist. Perhaps they're inherently bad people. Either way, it's a bit depressing and I probably won't talk about it much more. The other thing I don't like is the generally accepted attitude to litter. A few times I've asked someone if they have a bin and they've taken my rubbish from me and flung it into the air – as if I couldn't have done that myself. A few other times I've gone through a whole village where the only bin was in the Magazin Mixt and it was closed. At one point, when I was in the hills a bit, I tried unsuccessfully to explain to someone that I wanted to throw away my rubbish. I had the bag in my hand which contained a beer can (I spend almost all my time sober, in case you think I'm turning into an alco-pilgrim). At first the woman whose yard I was standing in thought I wanted beer, then wasser, then apa (both of them mean water). I kept doing an impression of me throwing it away and making a swishing sound which is what throwing something away would sound like if it made a sound but she refused to understand. After a while I noticed that in her yard, all round my feet, was a miniature pooscape: plastic bottles, dirty tissues, unidentifiable crud everywhere. I looked at my carefully packed selection of rubbish which I had carried for a few miles and back to the floor and it occurred to me that there wasn't a way of translating what I wanted to say.

As a result of this attitude, the beautiful and breezy villages of Romania stay beautiful, but wherever the wind loses its energy there's a pooscape. In the less windy areas the common pasture which surrounds most places is the local pooscape. And it's really sad. In Bulgaria, I'm pleased to report, there are bins on the street for public use.

Stick

I have good news for you: the death crack in my stick which I reported on before has been dealt with, I think permanently. Another smaller split had developed at about 100 degrees clockwise and it looked and sounded like I was about to lose a fairly hefty splinter. The rest would surely have followed. Luckily I made friends with an alcoholic old man in a pub who took me back to his house to give me a place to sleep and loads of greasy food and, also, fixed my stick after much huffing and puffing with various pieces of hosepipe and tape. I slept in his kitchen and shared the night with a turkey and her chicks. The turkey was a model of good behaviour and I barely noticed her at all.

Bulgaria

You're probably wondering what Bulgarians are like. Well this is what they're like. Despite being accessorised by Abi, who clearly had a walletful of money, we were given food by five different people one day (Abi counted them because, I'm sad to say, to me it didn't seem a particularly big deal). On our second night we came across a farm in the middle of a totally straight and completely empty road. It turned out that it was a bank holiday which meant that they invited us in and piled tons of food in front of us and gave us loads of rakiya (Bulgarian for tsuika or palinka) and said, "Nosdrovay!" every few minutes and roared with laughter about all sorts of things and their dog attacked me but only my boot which has been designed with dog attacks in mind so I escaped unscathed. A delightful, educated and well travelled French-speaking couple took us in and chatted away about Bulgarian history and their time in Algeria and the problem of Gypsies. The wife, Zoia, said, with a wink and a series of nods which could have meant, "This is a joke," "I think Hitler...ahhh...maybe had the right idea...tak tak tak." The "tak tak tak" was said while she was doing an impression of someone looking down the sights of a gun and shooting people.

I have slept indoors half the time since I've been here and today, a mere five days after May Day, appears to be St. George's Day. A celebration which apparently is just as serious as Easter – or, at least, they've killed a lamb and we'll be eating it for lunch.

Bulgaria

May 17, 2009

St. George's Day

The last few weeks have been pretty festival rich. First there was real Easter which the Orthodox people called Flower Day, then there was Orthodox Easter which was significantly better because there was tons of food and weird midnight masses with candles on the street and then Gypsies dancing round fires in the middle of back streets till morning and then more church with special crumbs of stale blessed bread which I got to take with me and red eggs aplenty and everyone saying, "Christ is risen! He is risen indeed!" to each other. Then a little later there was the First of May which involves huge piles of meat being shoved in front of you and rakiya (this was in Bulgaria) and everyone shouting "Nostrave!" every twenty seconds and just when you thought you'd for sure brought on a bout of bad belly with all the food and chillies and such, someone would say, "Would you like a pork steak?" and you'd have to look confused and say as sternly as you can, "No! I would not. I'll die if I have any more to eat."

So that's quite a lot of festivals if you ask me and if I was organising it I'd lay off for a while – but not the Bulgarians. The next one I got to was just after Abi left, St. George's Day. I arrived after dark and went up to the first people I could find and said, "Do you speak English?" and someone was quickly produced who was then quickly replaced by Lyubov, who is something like an English teacher (she's a biology teacher, but her English is pretty good) and Lyubov offered me something to eat and a bed. And, obviously, rakiya. Her family had a small dispute which Lyubov explained to me was about the lack of shower facilities in my accommodation. I explained about how delicate my crusty nubbins of dead foot skin are and that they need to be kept as dry as possible and everyone seemed happy with that. Also, Lyubov's father-in-law, Yoto, turned out to have done a pilgrimage round India. Around the coast, as far as I could tell, in two months. Which sounds preposterously fast but I think he used some trains. Anyway, he did it with his cousin who is a serial pilgrim. He pilgrims across one country and then when he gets to the end of it he saves up a bit of money by getting a job or something and then flies to the next destination to start pilgrimaging again. Obviously he's a nutcase.

At some point in the conversation Yoto said, "Tomorrow we're going to sacrifice a lamb for St. George's Day. Would you like to join us for the feast?" I said words to the effect of "Yes" and then he said, "Would you like to see the slaughter?" Would I? Would I ever! It was brilliant. I know how I'd slaughter a lamb and it is almost exactly the opposite of what happened. My method would be to chase it around for ages with a knife and eventually get round to cutting it a bit and then get grossed out and bottle it and there would be a bleeding lamb wandering around for a bit and then I'd hack open the middle and get covered in a big mash of goo and end up with some legs and some ribs and a massive pile of gunk and quite a lot of gunk all over me.

But what actually happened was different. The guy came out carrying a lamb and hooked its leg on a hook. Before I could wonder whether the hook was actually going through the leg or not (it was, I think) he'd whipped out a knife and cut the lamb's throat. About seven seconds later it was dead and he'd already started work on the legs. Once the skin was off the legs he hooked both the legs up and took the fleece off, which didn't seem to require a knife, he just peeled it. Throughout the procedure a sly nod to his son indicated that something should be washed so that at no point did anything get any kind of dirt on it for more than a second or two. A subtle cut somewhere and he was pulling out strings of intestine or something and coiling them in some way, then strings of another intestine and coiling them differently, then a couple of nicks on the kidneys released a bit more blood which had been hiding there, another intestine coiled differently again, a tiny grommet or gizzard or something was detached and thrown to the chickens. Another intestine (I decided after a while that probably some of them weren't intestines, but who knows?) needed a separate piece of equipment to clean it properly – a little bit of plastic tube which the guy blew down to clear the pipeway. I think the whole thing took about 20 minutes, by which time there was a pot of clean innards, a plate of innards which needed further cleaning by the lady folk, a neatly folded carcass and a fleece. The chickens only got a cup of blood and a finger-sized flubula.

Next everything was transferred to the girls who were totally prepared. A pot with some stuff in it was ready to accept one batch of guts; onions and rice and other things were ready to go with another batch for the stuffing. When they'd done their bit the stuffed lamb was put (with the head next to it) in a sort of outdoor oven. The fire had been going since the night before and it was dug into the ground, some embers were taken out and the lamb was put in. Then it was covered and the embers put on top and left for four hours.

Maybe I've given slightly too much detail there but I was pretty impressed by the whole thing. I have never killed any of my food and I reckon I know quite a few people who've never even seen their food alive. I didn't quite work out in what way it was a sacrifice but they told me it was one, so I suppose it was.

They sent me off with a load of lamb and innard stuffing (incidentally, this is delicious) and told me that since they'd been celebrating St. George a day earlier than usual I might find someone else who would invite me to their feast. They were not wrong. Feasts are so cool. I was just walking past someone's house when they shouted at me from the door to come over and then it was all lamb, stuffing and rakiya all over again.

Gypsies and Storks

I stayed with another family of Gypsies the other day. While we were eating supper the guy said, "Hey look," and a stork, of which there are plenty round these parts, flew past. About half a second later the self-same stork ploughed into the overhead electric cables. It was incredible. There was a small display of fireworks, a certain amount of flapping and then two dead ends fell to the ground and the stork flew off, alive. After the appropriate emergency service was alerted a van drove up and turned the whole village's power off and then drove away again. The stork won that battle.

Drunks

I've been on the receiving end of a fair bit of hospitality from drunk people. The good thing about them is that they're friendly and fun (or hostile and boring, depending) but I've begun to be slightly wary of believing everything they say. I followed an excellent yellow (on the map) road to the point where it turned white (on the map). There I found that instead of carrying on to Turkey, someone had dumped a massive industrial quarry thing on top of it. The road had been buried. Luckily there was a totally isolated little house by a lake full of roaringly drunk Hungarians who liked nothing better than to shout at each other. One of them spoke German and told me that I could stay the night and have dinner and such, and since I had no food with me and the prospect of retracing my steps for 5 kilometres was so depressing I thought, "Why not?" Especially since he made this proposal after I'd drunk some rakiya, which rarely has the effect of speeding me up. After dinner my German-speaking friend went home and so did everyone else except the owner, who then hoofed me out. Unfortunately my Bulgarian is still totally useless so I couldn't even say, "But your friend told me I could stay here." The story ends happily – I didn't die or anything and I even had a back-up plan (sleeping in my tent, as usual).

Kit

You know my trousers which you were worried about? It turns out that you had good reason. Just after I'd patched the knees both legs tore again just above the patches. I was halfway through patching the new holes (with the lower legs from my jeans) when Galin gave me some new trousers. I was sorry to let all my sewing go to waste but I have to admit that the new ones have certain advantages. Abi forced me to take two pairs of socks from Mum and she took four pairs off me, one of which was unused. I now have four pairs again, two unused, and today I had to forcefully reject a further pair. People will just not believe that I have enough socks. I'm wearing new pants and have jettisoned my Calvin Klein pair which I thought were inappropriately trendy. And had holes in. It's a struggle not to take jackets and jumpers, but since it is roastingly hot I have so far managed it. I've exchanged my two half-litre water bottles for one 2 litre bottle, leaving the other pocket on my bag free for booze. At the moment I've got about 75cl of rakiya and half a litre of wine. I exchanged most of my books with Abi for Le BGG – the French version of The BFG. Speaking of which, I mentioned before that the BFG was an allegory for the dangers of prejudice. It is not. The BFG, the only good giant, is white with a Big Friendly Roman nose. The others – the Bloodguzzler, etc – are all dark brown and have flat African noses and big lips. They wear a sort of primitive tribal outfit – a kind of small kilt or something – and nothing else, whereas the BFG wears a jacket and trousers which don't quite fit, in the manner of an eccentric Oxford don. What I meant to say was Sneetches on Beaches, I don't think there's any underlying racism in that.

I met a man who was pretty old and who replaced conversation with showing me round his workshop. He was some sort of metal worker. It seemed like there would be no obvious conclusion to his tour so I got him to sharpen my penknife. It's now supersharp. I also acquired another juju to go with my holy water. It's a rock. I think it's from a monastery in Greece. A rock. People in the army put rocks in their rucksacks and that's why everyone else laughs at them.

There's a possible problem developing with my tent, but I'll wait to see what happens before making too much of a big deal about that. Certainly it's not a death crack, but maybe one day it will be. I also gave my blow-up mattress to Abi and my back is beginning to get better as a result of all the weight I'm now not carrying.

Things I Haven't Mentioned

I haven't mentioned loads of stuff that's happened to me. I haven't mentioned Stefan with the tattoos on his face who saw me on the street and said, "Hey man, you wanna smoke a joint with me?" I haven't written about the time I went to the church which I'd camped behind and how I was walked up to the icons by a helpful person who grabbed my arm so I couldn't help but kiss them – nor about how I thought I'd sneak out for a few minutes to pack my tent away and how loads of people followed me and made me go and have lunch with someone else because they were worried that if they let me out of their sight I might run away without lunch. I haven't said anything about the guy I spoke to who had escaped from Bulgaria in the Communist days by watching where the soldiers walked and then making a dash for it at night. I haven't talked about the Romanian town I came across (in Bulgaria) where they all stared and shook their heads like the Romanians always did, nor about how Bulgarians seem to do a lot less staring and have running water everywhere nor about the huge amount of "cheese" and spring onions I've been eating nor about the woman who gave me a load of cheese under her husband's instructions and then, when he'd gone, scuttled back and gave me a bit more with a conspiratorial wink – nor about how I climbed Mount Shipka, nor about the huge amount of warning I was given against taking a white road through the mountains (Stefan: "It'll take you a week and you'll get lost"; Yoto: "Do what you like, but life is precious"). There're other things I haven't written about too, but I just can't write them all.

Halfway There

May 17, 2009

I haven't done a very thorough analysis of globes and routes and such recently but I reckon I'm halfway there. I've been telling people that the whole thing'll take me eight months but also that I don't really know. I've taken four months so far and if I've cleared about half the distance then I'm roughly on target for being right. Anyway, at what I think might be the halfway point, here is an abstract and reflective blog entry.

Getting Home

I have two ideas at the moment. I think it's most likely that I'll hitchhike back home, hopefully via North Africa and Spain. That would mean I'd get to go to Africa which I haven't done before and, as everyone knows, a circular route is best. My other plan is to sail back. I'd like to sail back a lot, but I doubt I'll be able to because I've tried to catch rides on boats before and failed, and I'm no better equipped this time.

Syria

Another thing that's on my mind at the moment is Syria. Lucas, the German bike-pilgrim who is following a similar path to me, tells me that Syrians will only let you into their country if you have a visa and they'll only give you one of them by sending it to your address. So that would totally rule me out of the visa option. I can't help but feel that it's worth turning up at the border and trying my luck anyway but I have been thinking about alternatives just in case. One is to go through Iraq; another is to sneak across the border in the night or something. Not my favourite idea but it has a sort of appeal. Probably it would make a good story. The only other thing I can think of is to sail around and land wherever I can, in Lebanon or Israel, or any other place I can get a lift to.

God

I've also had a little more time to think about why I'm doing this and I still don't really know. Before Lent my brother wrote a sermon about what Lent was for and why you should fast. One of the things he said was that there isn't an obvious reason why you should do it, and I think that also applies to pilgrimage. One thing that I think both of them achieve is a kind of discipline. Army people spend a long time practising turning round at exactly the same time even though it's a skill that is totally untransferable to the battlefield or, in fact, to anything. The idea is that the soldier trains himself to take orders without thinking and to know that he is always expected to achieve a certain standard in the things he does. That way, on the battlefield, instead of questioning the order that has been given or wavering because he is scared, he does it and does it well. I think there are aspects of Christian life which parallel parade ground training, including going to church, fasting and pilgrimage. When you do any of these things, even if no one sees you doing it, you are telling yourself by the way you act, "My life is not for me." A pilgrimage doesn't achieve anything and it doesn't have a spectacular effect – well, it hasn't on me yet – but the more of these disciplines you build into your life, the better prepared you will be on the battlefield. Whatever the battlefield might be.

I Love Turkey

May 24, 2009

Turkish Border

I got to the Turkish border after dark and also after I'd met a couple of Polish hitchhikers who told me I'd need €10 to get a visa. Naturally I didn't believe them, but if I had believed them I didn't have an alternative plan. I had with me 2 Lev which I'd been given by the Orthodox church along with a pretty classic selection of items. In total there was: a packet of biscuits, a loaf and a half of bread, a tray of weird Bulgarian sweets, 2 Lev (less than a quid, I think), half a litre of red wine in a Sprite bottle and, my most inappropriate gift yet by some distance, a kilo of white flour. The woman told me that I could mix it with water and make bread on a fire. I'm yet to do that.

Thus armed, I headed through the Bulgarian border control where I met two German horse couriers. I discovered that horse delivery is the most painful job in the world. They had been stuck at the border for a few days, waiting for some papers for something or other with only border police for company. The previous day, one of them had gone to Istanbul for something and the other had to stay behind without a passport in case he ran away and so he was stuck in the no-man's-land between the two countries where there are no shops or anything. And then, when they aren't being hassled by officials being official, they're hassled by officials being corrupt. Apparently if you turn a Turkish speed camera off and then on again it comes up saying 88, so lots of people who drive trucks in Turkey get speeding tickets for driving at 88km/h in a 50 zone. And they had their petrol cap stolen by the petrol guy. I met them because as I walked past one of them shouted, "Hey, Jerusalem?" and I had to admit that he was right.

Begging

And then it turned out that I needed €15 for a visa and the guy wouldn't back down and just give me one even when I looked up the Turkish word for "beg" in my dictionary and read it to him. In fact, I was ejected from the borderzone at 11pm and went to sleep in Bulgaria among a strip of petrol stations and parked lorries. Luckily I used the ejection time to think up a brilliant plan. In the morning I headed back into the borderzone with a piece of A4 paper saying, "I need €15 for a visa," and sat down next to a friendly control and begged. The Germans had given me about a pound in Euro and Lira coppers, so I put all that with my 2 Lev in my neckerchief (another use for a neckerchief) and waited. After a couple of hours a busload of Bulgarian women filed up one by one and dropped a coin into my pile and I was up to 4.20 Lev, 50 Euro cents and 75 Lira cents. Then after another half an hour someone in a coach gave her tour guide €15 to give to me. That pretty much did it. I was ecstatically happy. At 12.30 I was in Turkey and grinning like an imbecile at everyone in the filthy queue of traffic I was weaving through and offering anyone I saw a biscuit.

Turkey

You're probably wondering what Turkish people are like. Or maybe I gave the game away with the title? Too obvious, perhaps? I tried to just write "Turkey" but I couldn't stop myself writing "I love" on the front. One thing that has happened to me is that I walked past a petrol station and someone who worked there beckoned me over and said, "Chai? Chai?" and of course I said, "Yes." So we sat down and had tea the Turkish way, which involves drinking it from funny glasses with loads of sugar and also starting with half a cup of really stewed tea and adding half a cup of hot water. Except that whole thing happened about a million times. Petrol stations, old men outside cafés, reception booths of factories, a fronting workshop, security desks. There's no building I have walked past where I thought it was unlikely that someone would beckon me over to offer me tea.

Sometimes tea isn't available to the friendly person so they have to make do with what they have. In the cars they have horns and I'd say that about 2% of cars that drive past me beep their horn or flash their lights and when I look up they want nothing more than to wave and grin. And they have a special way of beeping which doesn't sound nasty and aggressive like the beeps in England do. They just do a couple of light mips so instead of "NYARRRG!" or "BRAAP!" it comes out like "Mippip!" and you can't really object if someone says Mippip to you.

Turkish Children

Another thing that happened to me is that I walked past a school playground full of 8-year-olds and they all bounded over to me and said, "My name is Mahmet," and, "Where do you from?" and, confusingly, "I love you." That's what the young school children are like. A little bit later I walked past a high school or something and a bunch of 15-year-olds were leaning out of the third storey window and they beckoned me over. Since it was impossible for me to come over I stepped towards them a bit and then shouted, "But you're up there," and then they belted down the stairs and appeared next to me and ushered me in and up the stairs and into the classroom and apparently their teacher had told them to fetch me so I could take the lesson. So I stood at the front and answered questions. Everyone was pretty excited to see me and it was with much rejoicing that I accepted the offer of school lunch. In the dining room the whole school got to check me out and I felt a bit like I'd just come out of the Big Brother house and had to suddenly deal with unearned fame. I think I mentioned at one point that I had no money and the children later spontaneously did a whip-round and produced 6 Lira in coins which I failed to turn away. I'm not normally particularly excited by being given money and giving it away a little bit later seems like a fair thing to do with it, but this was a bit more touching and I think this time I'll buy myself a present. My plan is to stay for a day or two in Istanbul and I reckon I can live on 6 Lira and a bag of flour for that long, so then I can tell the kids that they bought me a holiday.

The Most Important Man in Turkey

When I was in Germania maybe two or three people stopped in their cars to offer me a lift – an average of about one a month. In Eastern Europe the average went up to maybe two or three a week. In Turkey I think the average so far has been more than one a day. I keep turning down lifts from people who bewilderedly say, "No, no, I'm going to Istanbul, get in." One such person was the most important man in Turkey. Well he might not be but he's got to be in the top ten. One of the first things he said to me was, "Do you drink? Alcohol? What do you want? I've got everything." So naturally I said, "In your car? You have every kind of alcohol in your car? Why?" And he said, "I own an alcohol factory. Actually the only alcohol factory in Turkey." So I said, "In that case I'll have a raki and Red Bull." He said, "Fine," and then he said, "I also have many other factories. And petrol stations. And I know the president. And we're building a hydrogen peroxide factory in Brazil and something or other in South Africa. And my grandfather was the president who's on all the money and I have 9000 employees." Well that was all well and good but I wanted to sit down and we were on the side of a main road with a petrol station in sight. I mentioned as much and he said, "Go to the petrol station after that, that's one of mine," but I wouldn't drive with him, so he drove there and waited for me. Since it was a couple of kilometres I kept him waiting for I reckon 20 minutes, which made me temporarily feel like the most important person in Turkey. When I got there he was sitting in front of a kind of banquet made entirely out of petrol station snacks.

Street Urchins

On the other end of the scale of flashy jobs I also met a bunch of boys who were selling mops and brushes on the street. When I met them, they were all sitting on cardboard boxes with no shoes on eating bread and chocolate spread and some other kind of spread, possibly vanilla, from huge tubs. And, naturally, drinking tea. They beckoned me over and it was moments before I had a loaf covered in flavoured sugary goo in front of me and a chai in my hand. After I'd eaten they played a game where they made me say things, one of them being, "Lahr ilahi illallah, Muhammeden Resulallah" which means I've been tricked into becoming a Muslim. Not the first time that has happened, in fact. A security guard at a factory had already played the same prank on me the night before and, when it was successful, went into a slightly unnerving dance which he did while shouting and singing the creed. They're certainly all very Muslim round here.

Good Deed

I was lured into some kind of textile factory at some point and introduced to Dr. Mehmet, the resident doctor who speaks a bit of English. He gave me some food (or at least he talked to me and then some food appeared from somewhere) and smoked a lot and then I set off on my way. The next day he spotted me at a petrol station when he was on his way to Istanbul so he sat down for a quick chat but he accidentally left his cigarettes behind. I nabbed them thinking they might make a good present for someone since everyone here smokes and Mehmet probably wouldn't see them again anyway. Then, later, a lorry pulled over on the other side of the road and the driver beckoned me over. I didn't recognise him but he said, "Dr. Mehmet" and since I'd only met one doctor in Turkey, I handed over the cigarettes and felt quite pleased with myself for having done a good turn. I just hope he doesn't get lung cancer as a result. Anyway, the lorry driver mysteriously had a wife and two children as well as some sort of cheesy pancakes in his lorry, and he gave me some, so the story has a happy ending.

Istanbul

I've reached a place where the sign for the beginning of the next town is also the sign for the end of the last town and I think it's going to be like that all the way to Istanbul and beyond. Camping is probably going to be harder for a few days but, by all accounts, the Asian side of Turkey is even friendlier than the European side. So I have only hope.

More of Turkey

June 6, 2009

Sleeping Rough

My general plan for sleeping is to start looking for a good camping spot towards the end of the day so that as it gets dark I'm all set up. One problem with this plan is that sometimes I say to someone something like, "Hey, can you help me?" and they say, "Yes, Yes," and give me some tea and I hang around hopefully but then a bit later something changes and it turns out that they can't help me after all. Then it's dark and I'm on my own again and that's not always perfect. When I was approaching Istanbul and so sort of in the middle of a massive stretch of urban spread that happened. I walked on for a bit until I found a bit of nicely mown grass which was in the middle of a massive intersection. There was a tree which provided a bit of shade from the surrounding street lights and I reckoned that the cars (which were visible in all directions) couldn't see me if I didn't put my tent up. I wasn't worried about not putting my tent up because I met these two Polish hitchhikers on the border who didn't even have a tent with them, just roll mats, so I knew that tentless sleeping was a legit option. There's a fine line between camping and sleeping rough, and I think if you don't put your tent up you cross that line but I'm not a snob so I plopped down my sleeping bag, shifted my neckerchief over my eyes and went to sleep. Not very much later two people who weren't dressed as policemen woke me up by being next to me. It seemed that although I was quite well hidden from the passing cars, I was quite obvious to passing humans. They asked me some questions which I artfully managed to answer by saying, "Anlamiorum" (which means, "I don't understand") and then one of them got out his wallet and flapped it around and said, "Police. Passaport." I was just on the point of getting my passport out when it occurred to me that he might be doing that thing you see people do in films where they just pretend to be police and in fact aren't. And blow me, he was. I asked him for his ID again and he waved it more frantically than the first time. On the third ask he shook my hand and walked off. So I decided that I shouldn't sleep there, packed up my stuff and walked on.

A while ago Rory said that I should try sleeping in a graveyard and although I think he's a bit weird it certainly occurred to me that tonight would be a good night for it. And blow me, I then walked past a massive graveyard. Due to it being in a big city, real estate was sparse and the graves were absolutely crammed together with no space to walk between them and as a result I ended up sleeping on a grave. It was a surprisingly comfortable night – totally dark, no passing strangers, a double bed with non-spikey and quite squidgy greenery. And, most importantly, I wasn't woken up by a grieving widow in the morning. Still, I prefer the tent.

Istanbul

I had organised a place to stay in Istanbul with a couchsurfing guy and I had a kilo of flour in my bag and 6 lira in my pocket. All I needed now was to meet up with Lucas. You remember Lucas, he was biking to Tanzania and I met him in Austria. Well he took the long route and I took the short route and it looked like we were going to get to Istanbul at the same time, but I'd failed to meet him the day before and now we didn't have a plan. Lucas just said, slightly hopefully, "If we don't meet, I see you in Istanbul I think." And indeed I did see him, while I was walking along some little street in the city centre, heading towards Couchsurfing Omer's house. He said something like, "Ah, there you are." And then when I called Omer to say that there was two of me and one of me had a bike he said, "Ok, no problem." Well I made loads of pancakes, did a bunch of computering, no sightseeing, rested, ate, climbed a building, stayed with another couchsurfer on the Asian side, kept on walking, and several days of city later, I was out.

Tea

There's a right way and a wrong way to drink tea in Turkey. The right way is to have two teapots, the bottom one with hot water and the top one with superstrong tea in it, and they sit on top of each other. You also have a little vase-shaped glass with no handle and normally you have two lumps of sugar with it but sometimes you get to choose how much. Huge amounts of sugar are not frowned on. The wrong way is to not have any. Occasionally I have tea with a tea bag or from a glass which isn't the right shape but it's rare. The full two-pot apparatus can be found in pretty unlikely places. Yesterday I met a couple who claimed that they had broken down and needed 200 lira which they didn't have and had been waiting for two days. They had, in their car, the double teapot, gas cooker, quantities of tea, a box of sugar cubes and at least two glasses. I've been given tea by cherry-sellers by the side of the road, by countless security guards of factories and such in their little security boxes, road construction crews, café owners, café customers, all kinds of shop owners and petrol stations. Some petrol stations have urns with two taps (water and tea) where you can have free tea because, presumably, to deny the thirsty motorist their tea is something close to a human rights infraction. On the days when I've counted I've had: 14ish (lost count), 12ish (lost count), 7 (very hot day and this doesn't include the coke which the homeless guy bought me), and yesterday, 15. One day I'm planning to have a day when I accept every time someone offers me some tea but that will be a hard day I think.

Church

Church in Turkey is called Mosque and it's slightly different. I went for the first time yesterday having been too intimidated before. I thought I'd probably stick out a bit and do all the wrong things so I checked with someone who spoke English and found out the protocol. Thing one which is very important is not to be a girl. If I'd made that mistake I would have been very obviously out of place. The next thing is to wash loads of parts of your body which you don't normally wash, such as your feet and your forearms and hair. Since you put your socks back on after the foot wash it doesn't stop you smelling gross but possibly has some other health benefits. Then you take your shoes off at the obvious shoes-off bit, pick a spot, and surreptitiously watch some other people and copy what they do. It's pretty straightforward – you listen to the guy reading the Qu'ran for a while, then you all line up in lines and he carries on reading. Then everyone does a series of bows and kneels and at one point you all turn right and then you all turn left and then it's over. There are slight variations as well, like whether there's an imam at all and whether or not you have bead-time (which is when you take some statistic beads off the wall and work your way through them at high speed, presumably counting things). It doesn't take long and it's definitely worth it. There's something quite nice about it being all men too – I didn't get the impression that anyone was there just to meet girls, for example.

Turks

I was given some statistic beads a while ago. There are 33 of them on a bracelet and if you want to make statistics about cars which go past you, for instance, you can count 100 of them with three rounds of the bracelet (and you have to remember to add one more). I mention this because I said before that about 1% of cars which went past me beeped and waved and I know that as soon as you heard that you thought, "I wonder what the sample size was." I'm in the hills now with less cars around and more friendliness, making this the friendliest place I've ever been to by a stretch. Yesterday, in a sample of 33 cars, 6 beeped or flashed their lights to say hello and one stopped to give me a lift. The people I meet often take a photo of me with them. They take me by the arm if they're walking somewhere with me and they tell me that my eyes are beautiful. That is what we would have called Legendary Service when I was at Starbucks. However I have only really come across men. The women are there, going about their business, but they don't generally offer me tea or wave at me as they drive past or smile at me when I smile at them. Women just don't really feature in street life I think.

Bogs

Ages ago I remember this half-Turkish guy called Reg saying to me, "If you accidentally get poo on your hand, you wouldn't just wipe it off with a bit of paper, you'd wash it with water." His point being that there is more logic behind the Turkish system of post-poo clean-up than behind the English system. I thought about that for a long time and I couldn't see why he was wrong. Then I met Lucas who said, "You clean your ass with water, yes?" He'd been to India. It turns out that anyone who knows anything prefers the Middle Eastern way. When I got to Turkey I was confronted with the traditional hole-in-the-floor style bog, but instead of pink sandpapery loo roll, there was just a teapot of water. Avoiding as much detail as possible, the answer to Reg's 15-year-old riddle of why we wipe and don't wash is that you get your fingers covered in poo and that's just gross.

Mum

Mum is coming out to walk with me in about a week. She's something in the region of 69 now.

More Great Things About Turkey

June 17, 2009

Sleeping in a Church

One of Richard's plans was to sleep in a church at some point and I'm sad to say that the churches I came across were so universally defensive and unfriendly that after a while I stopped asking. The people I used to ask would say, "Not possible" in a way which made it quite clear that they really meant, "Please leave me alone, I don't like you and I don't want to help you." Even if there's a well-established rule that no one is allowed to sleep in the church, it's still possible if you get permission from the right people. Well anyway, I was just putting my tent up next to a mosque when someone came along and said that if I liked I could sleep inside and they had a sort of basement which had a load of tables, tea-making facilities (and tons of tea and sugar) and a folding sofa-bed. Naturally I was delighted. Then the guy said "Are you hungry?" and gave me a bunch of food and, of course, tea.

Mosque

I went to the mosque the other day when I was waiting for Mum to show up. I really like going to the mosque. Perhaps it's just because it's something unusual for me but there seems to be quite an honest atmosphere of reverence and holiness. The service or whatever you call it is both public and private – public in that you're all together and private in that the whole time everyone is whispering their own prayers to themselves at their own speed, nothing is said communally. When I came out someone who had met me at the café before asked me, a bit confused, if I was a Muslim. I said, "A little," which I think is fair. After all, I subscribe to the Lahr'illi illah uhl'Allah bit even if I haven't come round to the Muhammeden Resullullah section of the creed. After a bit of surprised chattering between themselves, one of them asked me what my Muslim name was. Busted: I didn't know I needed a Muslim name. I had to come clean. Still, they don't seem to mind me joining in.

Baths

I met Mum in a place called Hammamkirahisar or something. The Hammam bit at the beginning means "Turkish Bath" which they had one of and which I went to. Pretty cool – it's kind of a cave with a domed roof where a bunch of young men wearing pants lark around like children. I was trying to do my laundry by the side but it was made quite hard by a large Turk who kept challenging me to a wrestle. Bath wrestling involves putting the other guy's head under the water to win. There was also a massive powerful spout of warm water coming in from somewhere which you could amusingly kick/push someone in front of/spray at people/try to stand in front of without being knocked over. Also included was a long mobile-phone photo shoot.

Turks Again

The Turks are (among other previously mentioned good qualities) surprisingly playful. Did you know that? In my mind a Turk was a short furious man in a turban with a beard who shouts and spits and cuts people's heads off with a curvy sword. They're not like that at all. I often see pensioner-aged men grabbing some friend's item of clothing just to annoy them or doing some other idiotic and light-hearted thing. I saw one fifty-year-old pick up a seventy-year-old in his arms and run over to a pond to pretend to drop him in. That sort of thing lifts the spirit in the same way that seeing a young child being gracious or hospitable does.

Inappropriate Gift

I have a vague feeling that I was not particularly flattering about the kilo of flour I was given. Yes, I had to carry an extra kilo of weight for about 9 days but in the end I managed to turn it into pancakes which, after all this time, are still probably my favourite food if they haven't just been overtaken by curry. And to put it in perspective I was given about 2 kilos of soap the other day. I stopped at a container ship dock where the manager welcomed me in and introduced me to his sub-managers before their managers' meeting. They were all quite pleased to have me in the office and as a token of their esteem they gave me what I suppose is the standard gift pack. It contained: toothpaste (I was about to run out); a sort of cologne that they splash around all over the place round here and which has been quite useful for neutralising my feet without water; a mystery cream; a tube of shaving cream; a bottle of what I at first thought was shampoo but which, after I'd squeezed it on my shirt to wash it, turned out to be "body yoghurt"; two different bars of soap which both "contained milk"; and two packs of four bars of soap. Ten soaps! And a whole host of hygiene products with dairy ingredients. Why? What could possibly be good about putting milk on yourself? Milk is the starting point of one of the foulest smells in the world. Well it all worked out quite well because I gave them all away quite quickly and even got some cherries in return for some of them.

Mum

Mum came to see me the other day. It worked out excellently. The Turks performed in textbook manner by springing tea on us all the time and feeding us despite Mum having a walletful of Euros. The route hadn't quite reached the massive flat boring plain that I think I'm about to cross and there were still some villages and such to break up the walking. She successfully hitchhiked home by using the often-frowned-upon hitching technique of paying someone to drive her to a bus station although, to be fair to her, we had spent 8 hours walking along a road and been passed by exactly three cars.

Sample Day

I can't write anything about most of the times people give me food or are nice to me in some way. There are way too many. To give you a flavour, this is what happened today. I woke up in a building site (they're building an intercity rail line from Ankara to Konya), had breakfast with the builders (fried egg, bread, olives, tomatoes, two cups of tea – pretty standard). As I approached a village a guy on a motorbike stopped to say that he'd give me a lift to the café where he'd buy me a tea. I walked to the café and he bought me a tea. Two teas, in fact. I had lunch by myself – bread given to me by the builders, boiled eggs given to me the day before by some other guy, chocolate spread and cheese left for me by Mum. On to the next town where two people who were guarding a factory gave me a cup of Nescafé (already poured out, presumably for one of the two) but they couldn't help me with the internet. In town (Sülüklü, marked on my small map of Turkey as being one of the notable towns of the area – population 3000) I asked for a place where I could use the internet for free and now I'm in an internet café, not paying and the guy who is in charge has given me a cup of tea and then asked if I want to stay at his house tonight. I have said yes.

Route

From Captain Andrew to Istanbul I followed the E5 (pr. "ehbesh") which is a big filthy main road which goes through a handful of massive cities and a whole load of factories. I was braced for it being grim and it turned out to be great, thanks to Turkish people being awesome – like Nizam, who let me sleep in his plastics factory. Then I left the E5 at İzmit, headed into the mountains, met mum at Hamamkarahisar, and now I'm heading for a massive salt lake called (in Turkish) Saltlake. And after that, Syria.

Pilgrims in Turkey and Other Things

July 4, 2009

Breathless Summary

I'm going to have to breathlessly summarise what I normally would have spun out over several pages because I've got an exciting headline article to put in and it's going to take up all the space. What you're missing out on includes, among other hilarious highlights, the two full days of passing only liquids and passing a fair quantity of those liquids combined with the amusing squatty Turkish lavs and my total lack of balance at the best of times and my toe blisters and boots and stomach upheaval making it not at all the best of times balance-wise. Also the heat went from blistering to sweltering as I went over a mountain which protects most of Turkey from the humidity caused by the sea, meaning that I now wear intra-cheek padding – lav roll or equivalent, which isn't easy to find (seems like most of the paper around here is made entirely out of water) – as a standard when walking to prevent the blistering of my bottom and at night if I put my tent up it's way too hot and if I don't put it up then I get attacked in a most unpleasant way by mosquitoes (and it's way too hot) which situation would be excellently summarised by the Turkish phrase: I spit up, there's a moustache, I spit down, there's a beard. It includes a single game of backgammon which accounts for all the game playing I've done in Turkey despite the fact that the nation is founded on chai and games, a single game of backgammon which was played at lightning speed and where, if I took longer than a second to move, my opponent moved my pieces for me. It includes a game I played with a newly-literate man who didn't know quite how to use a dictionary. He borrowed my dictionary and flicked through it, occasionally finding an interesting thing which he would then read the English of but he read the English as a Turk would read it, phonetically and with a few crucial differences – c becomes a soft j like in jardin, etc. His interests were wide-ranging and due to the nature of the game, totally non-sequiturial and he wouldn't let me read what it was he was trying to read but I managed to work out letoojay zhoojoombeh. Maybe that story would be funnier if you could hear it. Doesn't matter because it's a story I'm not going to tell you because it's come into the breathless summary instead of the main section, not unlike the time when I was converted to Islam for like the 5th time but this time I was given a Muslim name – Abdullah – so now I'm for real. Also the time a sneaky cloud with a storm in it surprised me from behind a mountain and I arrived at the next petrol station with a small dry patch on my pants and everything else wet (an interesting reversal). Gosh, I'm running out of breath and I haven't even mentioned all the bad things that have happened like when I had to pack up my tent again because the local kids turned on me and one spat on my tent and I thought I've had enough of this or the other time when I put my tent in the garden of a mosque and then went off to have dinner and came back to find it totally overhauled with all my stuff everywhere and thought my camera had been stolen except it hadn't been stolen, it'd just been used by my retarded assailants to take photographs of the pillage (and each other) although that turned out to be quite a good thing later, or all the times when children say Money Money to me which always makes me feel sick or the girl who answered the door when I knocked and literally screamed and ran back inside although that also turned out to be a good thing later because that family gave me dinner and breakfast and loaned me a blanket. Did I ever say about the time I was offered a lift by two boy-racers which I turned down of course and as they drove past they made fun of me for going so slowly with the international, "You're plodding" signal, only they were driving a horse and cart? What am I thinking? That was in Romania. I can't start on stuff from that long ago now.

Wedding

If you're anything like me you'll probably have thought at some point, "When's he going to go to a wedding? Everyone who goes on a big journey gets invited to a wedding and normally they're the guests of honour and someone kills a pig for them or whatever, and he's been going for some time now and not a wedding in sight." Well you should have had more patience because as I was walking along the road somewhere near the massive salt lake someone stopped his car next to me and said, "My brother is getting married in the next village and I would be glad if you would come and be my guest." Well the next village turned out to be quite far away so I got there kind of late and missed most of it and there wasn't a pig sacrifice, I think partly because they were all Muslims but maybe because I was late. Anyway, it was cool. They all danced away with each other for ages to the dulcet slash foreign sounds of the tuberlele and four-stringed qatar and I talked to Ergun. He was the guy who stopped the car to talk to me. He turned out to be more interesting than most of the other people I meet and one of the interesting things he said was that he was interested in me because I'm free and he envied my freedom.

Freedom

That made me think a bit, and I'm always wondering why I'm doing this pilgrimage so it's always good when someone comes up with a new answer. I suppose it's obvious that I'm free – I feel as free as anything, I feel like I'm flying through life – but the stats are against me. Here are some of my shackles and chains:

- Shackle 1 – I have no money with me so I can't buy anything.
- Chain 1 – When I get given money I've made it my principle to always give it away instead of spending it on myself (I gave my 20 lira to a kid who gave me some cherries the other day).
- Shackle 2 – I'm 2500 miles away from home.
- Chain 2 – I'm walking to Jerusalem.
- Chain 3 – I've decided not to accept any lifts in cars if they're offered to me.
- Shackle 3 – I have to carry all my stuff.

There may be some others but I don't want to bang on. My point is that if this were a punishment it would be a pretty bad one and I would be one of the less free people. As it is, I chose it all and because I chose it my freedom shines out of me and into passing cars.

Ergun

Well I naturally told him that if he wanted he could come and walk with me and he said, "Yeah, but I've got a wife and stuff," and I said, "Yeah, fine, well if you change your mind here's my email address." Just before I got to Adana I got an email from him saying that he was in Adana and that I should tell him where I was so he could come and find me. In the end we settled on meeting in Adana at the Sapanca Mosque (built by a guy called Sapanca who modestly named it after himself) where he said he would wait for me. A pretty unlikely story, but I'm a trusting soul and I couldn't see the harm in trying to find him. After dark I was just about to give up since he clearly wasn't there and I was heading off to find an internet so I could write him an email saying, "You weren't there so I ditched you," when I found him. He was sitting on the lawn with two friends a little way away from the Mosque and I suppose he hadn't seen me before. Anyway it turned out that his friends were just people he'd met from sitting there, he'd been there since 3pm, he had with him a napsack, a sleeping bag and a flute and when I asked him where he was sleeping tonight he said, "I don't know – wherever you're sleeping." He was genuinely coming with me. In fact I think he was only in Adana in the first place to find me. All this I realised afterwards.

Co-Pilgrim

I couldn't have been more delighted. I remember Richard saying ages ago that he hoped we'd pick up some fellow pilgrims but I didn't think any would really come. Ergun said he was coming to the Syrian border with me at which point he'd have no passport and would have to go home. That's a week at least! We stayed at the Muslim community centre which his new friends were somehow involved with and the next day we were on the road.

Five clicks later disaster struck in the form of Ergun's grandfather dying which meant he had to turn and flee. So in the end he didn't come that far with me, but what can you do? There's no convenient time for a grandfather to die.

Another Pilgrim

Later I was ambling along and a vanful of people stopped by me and said, "You are going to Kudus?" (Kudus is what they call Jerusalem.) I said, "Yes, I am," and they said, "You come to our house, there is French man pilgrim go to Kudus by walk, we take you." I said, "I'm only walking," and they said, "Yes, you like walk. Andre say always he like walk too. Ok."

Sure enough, here, at their house is Andre who has walked from France taking roughly the same time as me and a totally different route. He also has a hazel stick and in fact he claims that when he saw it in the woods it made him think, "I should walk to Jerusalem with that." He's been to the Syrian border, he's put my border-crossing plan into action (ask for a visa and then when they say no just wait until they change their minds) and he's been rejected. Now he's been staying with this family for 9 months.

Dictionary Game

Did you work it out? I'll give you a clue – he was reading the entry for "salata".

The Last Part of Turkey

July 13, 2009

Andre's Story

I walked for a while along a section of road which would have been called Pilgrim Alley if it had been in America. I met a bunch of pilgrims there. One English guy on a bike, two Spanish people who were biking to Jerusalem and Andre, the French guy who had had trouble with the Syrian border. Before he got to Syria he was set about by two ruffians who were driving a horse and cart. They lurked in the bushes for him for a couple of hours while he had loads of chai at a petrol station and then when he walked past they did a drive-by jacket robbery. Well Andre had probably been singing the second verse of Bunyan's awesome hymn – the bit about, "He'll with a giant fight" so he wasn't afraid of two measly little ruffians and he attached himself to their cart. Sadly it only resulted in him getting a chestful of gravel and a bump on the chin but on the plus side he was taken in by the family whose factory he was opposite at the time. After he had been rejected by the Syrians, aggressively and with insults, he ambled mournfully back towards France and when he got to the family they ushered him in.

For some reason they told him that they would pay for his flight back to France when they had the money and also that they would sort out his visa problem. The problem was that by the time they gave him the money his visa had run out by several months. In a most peculiar turn of events he was fined $400 on exit and since he only had $300 they said he couldn't leave. They forced him to stay in Turkey without a visa. So he went back to the family and is now waiting for them to buy him a boat ticket to Cyprus and from there to Lebanon.

The Spaniards

Pilar and Nacho biked past me and since we were all heading for Jerusalem we stopped and had a chai and since we were all hungry they bought me lunch. They told me that there was a monastery in Eskanderun where I could stay for free and I noted that mentally and then they boosted off at a gentle pace. Three days later I got to Eskanderun and started asking people for a monastery. They all started helpfully saying, "Yes, you want the church, it's down here, come with me, I'll show you," so I had to fight them quite hard in my best Turkish (which is pretty excellent by now, in case you're wondering) to make them admit that there was a monastery. And in the end they won and didn't admit it so I settled for going to the church.

When I buzzed on the buzzer a woman said, "Yes?" and I said, "Do you speak English?" and she said, "Turkish," so I said, "Um, ok, me pilgrim…man speaking…priest have you?" (in Turkish) and the door buzzed open. There was a bunch of youths playing volleyball and from somewhere a woman who was plainly the owner of the voice emerged and eyeballed me. I smiled in a way which I thought would persuade her to let me stay for a night and started again: "I Jerusalem pilgrim…two Español people speaking monastery…sleeping here me one night…" and just as I was about to crumble under the power of her stare, Pilar and Nacho appeared and hugged me. After our emotional reunion I turned back to the grumpy guardian and said, "This! This people…" but she had started walking away by then.

Totally baffled, I followed the Spaniards towards another frosty old woman who snapped something in Italian at them and they said, "It's ok, you can stay here, we'll show you your room." That was smashing news. We went up some stairs and there was another icy matron who unlocked a door, dismissively handed me the key and then wandered off. The room was air-conditioned, had an adjoining shower/lav combo which they seem to have no qualms about putting in the same tiny area round here, and was in all respects a hotel room except that it didn't come with a toothbrush (I've lost my toothbrush). I'd come just in time for supper which was delivered in the same style as everything else. The nuns or sisters or whatever they were ate somewhere else, the food was just left on the table for the guests (just me and the Spaniards) and it was delicious and plentiful. Breakfast the next day was the same. I think the whole experience was the least friendly and highest quality of my whole journey. Nacho and Pilar had been there for three nights or so and it seemed that they hadn't spoken to anyone for more than a sentence either.

Syrian Border

After hearing Andre's story I adjusted my plans mildly. The first change was to take a slight detour which took in two different border crossings to double my chances of getting across. The second change was to practise telling people that I was heading for Damascus – a lie that is not altogether untrue. I got to the Turkish border quite late in the day, had some small interactions with the Turkish chaps involving a certain amount of pointless wandering around and then I was officially dismissed from the country. For some reason the Syrian border is about 4km away through a barren no man's land and when I got there it was dark and I was exhausted. The soldiers whose job it is to lurk around drinking tea all welcomed me most cordially with such phrases as "Welcome in Syria" and "I love you" and I thought – this is going to be a breeze. I found a place which was obviously selling visas and presented myself to the police. Pretty much all of them looked at my passport before I was ushered into a small office and told I could have a visa for $25. Bargarooni. I said I only had 51.10 Lira (I'd found 1.10 on the road) and they said actually it was $52 and they didn't accept Lira because they are Syrians. Then I was escorted into another office where I presumed a more important person would say, "Just let him in Mehmet and stop being so officious." Actually it was officious Mehmet himself in the more important office and he didn't like the look of me one bit, so I was taken to the army guys and driven back to Turkey. My escort said I couldn't come back even if I came back with the right money tomorrow and that if I wanted a visa I should go to Ankara. Disappointing news.

The people in the restaurant in the Turkish customs were hateful to me and wouldn't give me water for free and then I found a nice person who said I could put my tent on some grass and some other nice people who gave me sweets. In a customs place! So I slept and I made a plan. The plan was this: if I went back to Syria twelve hours later there would almost certainly be no one there who would recognise me because no one does more than a twelve-hour shift. So I changed my Lira (I got $31 for it so I was most of the way there) and I found the friendly guy from the night before. While I checked on the internet to see how badly I'd been ripped off (not badly at all) he made an excellent sign for me which said something like, "I need $70 for a visa please." I had told him $52 but he thought I might need some money for food as well. And then he bought me breakfast.

While I was eating breakfast someone came along and nabbed my sign and wandered off with it. When he came back he had 6 Lira and then a little later he had another 5. I scribbled out $70 and wrote $21 and then scribbled that out and wrote $14. Before I'd finished eating another guy came along and told me to follow him. He took me to the money exchange place, I threw in my Lira with his pile and he handed me $71. I said, "No, no, I only need $52," and he said something about how Turkish people are hospitable and I ended up keeping the $71.

My plan worked perfectly. No one knew who I was at the Syrian place in the morning and I found a friendly Turkish guy who translated for me and was generally helpful. They did say things like, "Why have you got this big 'Cancelled' stamp in your passport from last night?" and when I told them it was a money problem the big cheese was again consulted.

Luckily it wasn't Mehmet and he saw no problem in letting me in. A whole bunch of paperwork later and I have a totally illegible visa which lasts for I don't know how long and cost me $52. And I walked into Syria. Here's what I learnt – the Syrian border people don't like people who are going to Jerusalem and they don't like poor people, so if you're a poor Jerusalem-bound pilgrim hoping to cross Syria, practise lying truthfully. And do your begging before you try the border.

The First Bit of Syria

July 19, 2009

Eggs and Chickens

If you're following my journey with mild detached curiosity you might have the idea that I've got a long way to go. I've done some calculating and also some chicken counting and I reckon I'm pretty much almost there. I'm definitely on the home straight, that's certain, and I think it's all flat and a total breeze from now on and maybe there's a touch of desert in the way and some border controls but to all that I say Ptsch and I think I'll be in Jerusalem in three weeks or so. Now I'm in Homs or Hims or Hums or something which means I'm already on the second half of my Syrian map.

Syrians

But you're probably wondering what Syrians are like and there's me not telling you. They're like this – last time I wrote I had been looking for a place with the internet when someone stopped in his car and said, "Is there anything I can do to help you?" I said I was looking for the internet and I doubted that he could help with that and he said, "Here's a map to my shop in this town, we have the internet there, you can have some tea, etc." So I went there and, lo, the whole place was in the grip of a power cut and after an hour or so I reckoned that I could probably get to the next city before they fixed their electricity problems and I left. After not finding the internet a million times in all the places where I'd expect to find it in any other country (including a place called Future Technologies, but maybe the internet will get obsoleted in the future) another person stopped in his car and gave me a packet of biscuits and asked if he could help in any way. He then drew a map to his pharmacy and when I got there he asked if I was hungry and bought me a whole roast chicken and a pile of flat bread things and some hummus and salad and it was the kind of meal that would be sold as a Family Meal Deal in KFC or somewhere except it didn't come with 2 litres of Coke but instead 3 litres of tea. And they had electricity. Also what the Syrians are like is this – in Turkey I was constantly being waved over to someone so they could give me tea or whatever and here it happens even more. I've been walking down the main highway from Aleppo to Damascus which conveniently has another local road running next to it most of the time which has no traffic on it. Yesterday I spent a good portion of the day walking on the hard shoulder despite the available much safer and nicer road because I'm simply not able to avoid the constant barrage of good intentions. Everyone is insistent that I need a rest or if not that I come over and talk to them anyway. I've worked out that they're normally happy if I sit down for a few seconds and then get up and go but all that stopping and starting, I just don't have the energy. So I've been hiding on the motorway. Here's another thing they're like – when they've finished eating something which came in a packet they fling the packet into the air in the manner of a Romanian, meaning that the whole place is filthy. And another thing that they're like is that twice someone has given me a drink or something from their shop and then when I've drunk it they've tried to charge me for it. It's surprisingly like Romania in some ways except you can't draw an easy racial line between the good guys and the bad guys.

Caffeine

Tea is different here. They still drink tons of it but instead of having two teapots they only have one. And instead of me having control over how much sugar goes in, they put the sugar directly into the teapot. And instead of there being a normal amount of sugar, there's absolutely loads. Coffee is different too. Instead of coffee being nice, it tastes like acorns. The first time I had it I thought they'd run out but were too embarrassed to admit it because they gave me a tiny little droplet of coffee in the bottom of my cup. Then they poured another similar measure for everyone else and I realised that it was only possible to drink it in shots because it's so foul. And when I say it tastes like acorns what I really mean is that it's like being punched in the mouth by a massive acorn, it's so strong. I have about one or two shots a day.

Motorbikes

When I got to Romania I wrote in my book under the title, "Things I've Seen in Romania," "Three children on a motorbike." I now wonder about how that could have made any impression at all. I am often offered lifts by people on motorbikes, more than once by two people on a single motorbike. Yesterday I thought I saw five people on a bike but as they drove off I doubted myself. Then later I definitely saw six people. Six people on one motorbike. Two parents and four (pretty small) children in this order: Wife, child, child, father, child, child – the last of which was fairly well squashed against the handlebars.

Arabic

Turkey was so big that I'd almost forgotten what it's like to learn a totally new language with a different alphabet from scratch by complete immersion. It's getting easier. The best place to start is with hostile border police when you have a complicated and stupid history to tell them. I have since discovered that there are a bunch of Turkish words which are Arabic so I have a sneaky headstart. But really this country's so small that I'm not sure I can be bothered to put much effort into it. I'll be out of here in a week or two.

The Last Bit of Syria

July 30, 2009

Police

I had four encounters with the police in Syria, all of them bizarre. The first time I was introduced to their funny ways they stopped in their car while I was walking on the road and asked me for my passport. That's a bit unfriendly but not particularly surprising, but what I wasn't prepared for was how much they didn't look like police. There were five of them, two carrying machine guns, one wearing a towel round his head and the other two doing the talking. None of them had uniforms and the car was a battered rusty old non-police car. What they looked like, in fact, were terrorists. My first reaction was to go a bit shaky and then I asked for some ID which completely baffled them but eventually one of the talkers produced a laminated piece of paper with some Arabic writing on it which he claimed said Police. That totally didn't convince me, but they said, "Please?" and that made me think they probably were police so I gave them my passport. A quick look, a quick phone call, and they were on their way. I asked someone about it later and he said, "What, you want them to go out and buy costumes?" as if that was a totally unnecessary and namby-pambyish thing to do. He didn't think I'd been terrorised at all.

The second time I was staying with someone he got on the phone and said, "I need to take your passport to the police." So naturally I said, "My eye you do!" but he insisted and eventually persuaded me to hand it over. Apparently the town policeman had heard about me but couldn't be bothered to come and find me to hassle me so he did it remotely through my host.

The third time was the most bizarre. Someone by the road in a tent hailed me over for some tea. I went. A little later another guy came and sat down. He said after a little while, “Bassfor,” which I pretended not to understand so he said, “Police. Bassfor,” and so I said, “Yes yes, I have one,” and then when he carried on insisting (bassfor is Arabic for passport) I made him show me his ID which he did, incredibly grudgingly, and it was the same yellow as the other one I’d seen so I believed him. Then he wanted a photocopy and I was glad to be able to tell him that since we were several kilometres from the nearest town and I was walking, he couldn’t have one. He tried to persuade me to get on his motorbike (non-police) but I refused. A few minutes down the road I found him talking to an American guy on a bike who was similarly unconvinced that he should hand over his papers. I told him I thought it was ok and the policeman once again tried to persuade me to get on his bike. Then he told us to carry on, but we wanted to talk to each other, so we sat down in the shade. The policeman huffily drove off. Then he came back. And he just sat there next to us getting more and more impatient. Eventually he was sitting on his motorbike with the engine on, beeping his horn to get us to move and when I once again refused to get on his bike he couldn’t believe it. He drove off. He came back. He showed me the photocopy of David’s passport. He kissed me on the cheek, and blew kisses at me, and grabbed my arm and tried to pull me onto his bike. I wriggled free and carried on walking. For the next two or three hours he reappeared about ten times, every time suggesting that I get on his bike. I stopped for tea with two different people and he invited himself along both times. When I got to his town he drove along next to me and shouted at anyone who tried to talk to me so I’d get to the photocopier sooner. I really thought that when he had his photocopy he’d leave me alone but he didn’t. It was quite dark by the time I persuaded him to stop following me around and to do that I had to be quite stern.

Quite late that night I met a guy who said I could stay at his house, which was nice because finding a campsite in the dark is a drag. I went to his house and ate some food and then I noticed that my host (a 25-year-old guy) was crying about something and the more I ate the more I began to suspect that I was the cause of some problem. It turned out that the police had phoned his father (whose house it was) and warned him not to take me in, and although it wasn't against the law, he would have had to put up with a load of questioning the next day if I stayed. Or, probably, he had to anyway. That confused me because I knew the police by this stage, and had been kissed by them several times and he had insisted that his hounding me was for my safety and peace. Apparently it wasn't exactly the police who had interfered but something which is ironically called "The Intelligence." Goodness knows what "The Intelligence" thought I was going to do, but thanks to them I slept on a patch of dirt outside town instead of in a room.

Kit

- My boots have now got holes in both sides of both feet which means that the sweat can get out, so it's good.
- My shirt has a few small holes here and there but has resisted incredibly well considering I have worn it almost non-stop for more than 6 months now.
- I disastrously lost my rosary and my statistics beads, but luckily someone gave me some more. I think before I left I had probably said the Hail Mary less than 50 times in my life and now I think I have said it more than 10,000 times. That's from saying a rosary every day for about 200 days, though these days I use Muslim beads which makes me feel like a bit of a rebel.
- My tent is still intact though less used these days. My stick is the envy of everyone who likes sticks.
- I've read The Pilgrim's Progress and I'm reading it again. It's excellent. I'd recommend it. All the characters are called things like Piety or Honest (goodies) and Worldly Wiseman or Simple (baddies)

and at one point Faithful says about Talkative, "You would as soon trust a Turk as trust him." Which was a cool thing to read in Turkey.

- I still have the candle from the Romanian Gypsies which I'm to light in the Orthodox church and the page from Ghislain's saints book which he tore out for me.
- Since coming to Syria I have very rarely carried any food with me. People don't really offer it to me to take away and there's not really any need for it since there are always other people inviting me for a meal.

Monasteries

Nacho and Pilar, these two Spanish pilgrims I met, taught me about staying in monasteries and told me where to look. In Syria I stayed in four monasteries and on one church roof. I stayed in a huge convent in Saydnaya and spent an entertaining half hour talking to one of the nuns there who, between dashing off to fix the water problems and yelling, "La wehn?" (which means, "Where do you think you're going?") at any of the orphans who tried to sneak out, told me off for going to the mosque. It was Friday when I spoke to her and as it happened I'd been to an Orthodox mass in the morning, Friday nammas in some mosque at lunchtime, and Orthodox vespers in the evening. She also told me off for being a Protestant because we don't love Mary. She was cool.

Jews

One of the monks I came across asked me where I was going and then he said, "Don't say Jerusalem, say Jordan. People will know you're going to Jerusalem, but don't say it." I ignored his advice and I have definitely come across some hostility because I'm going to Israel. "Do you recognise Israel?" is a question someone asked me the other day, and most people say, "Ah, Philistine" when I tell them Jerusalem, as if Israel doesn't exist. I began to think that if I was a Jew I might have had quite a different experience in the Muslim world, but I'm glad to say that David, the American guy, said that everyone was nice to him. He said they always said, "Jews, Christians, Muslims – brothers," just like they say to me.

Jordan

As well as the preposterously large $52 visa for Syria, they also stung me with a leaving tax. What the heck is that? Leaving tax my foot. It was another $12, which left me five quid short for the Jordan visa. Luckily Jordan is a friendly country so I could say, "I'm going to Jerusalem and I don't have enough money for a visa and can I camp at the border because I'm tired?" and instead of them booting me out, they said, "Wilcom, wilcom," and somebody gave me the fiver I needed and I slept on the pavement outside the police building, a stamped visa in my passport and totally legal. Jerusalem in a week? I'm almost there.

Jordan to Israel

August 6, 2009

Jordan

You might be wondering what Jordanians are like but when I tell you that the last four days have been probably the roughest of the whole trip I'm sure you'll instantly stop caring and want to know about my suffering instead. So to briefly summarise so as to get more quickly onto the main attraction, they're super friendly like Syrians but without so much of the craziness and intrusiveness, so an improvement. If I had much of an appetite at the moment I'm sure I'd be eating well but as it is I'm eating adequately.

A Tough Day

After rolling cheerfully through Jordan for a couple of days I met a couple of young guys who spoke good English and liked walking. I stayed with them for a night and the plan was for them to walk with me the next day. In the night I contracted some sort of illness and by morning I was fevery and had done several watery poos. Not wishing to lose co-pilgrims or inflict myself on them for too long we set out at about 3 in the afternoon when I was feeling better but still pretty bad. One of them took my bag but even then I was dizzy and weak all day and it was all uphill. As soon as they left I found a place for my tent and deliriously set it up and then slept for 12 hours.

Insane Heat

After all that I arrived in the Jordan Valley, which in Arabic is called Al Gore. It is insanely hot. They say 40 degrees if that means anything to you. I'd say it like this – when I breathed in through my nose I sometimes got the burning feeling you get in a sauna and I also drank a ginormous quantity of water which went directly from my stomach to my back. I walked through this valley for a day and a half before I got to the King Hussein Bridge, which goes into Israel. When I got there it was closed. What on earth? You can't close a border. Or a bridge. They said it would open again at 8 in the morning so I slept on some cardboard boxes by the road. Way too hot for the tent, and way too hot for sleeping outside, but I found that if I woke up sweating then I could sit up for a bit and cool down enough to go back to sleep. As soon as the sun came up the flies, of which there are billions, swarmed in and tried to crawl into my mouth and other such orifices. That night I wasn't given any food so I ate a spoonful of marmalade for dinner. Not totally satisfactory, but the combination of heat and convalescing meant I wasn't very hungry.

Spilt Milk

In the morning I tried the bridge again. Five pound leaving tax! That is such a massive scam. A friendly guy paid for me. Then I wasn't allowed to walk across the bridge but had to take a bus instead, and that cost four pounds. Another massive scam. A friendly girl paid for me. Two hours later I was in Israel and shuffling bewildered through the uselessly organised Israeli border. I had to check my bag in for some reason and at every opportunity they took my passport and disappeared with it and gave it back haphazardly later. By 11 I had got past the preliminary screening and had been marked as suspicious and had to sit in a pen for suspicious people so they could interrogate me later. I don't know what it was exactly that made my female interrogator think I was dodgy. Our conversation went something like this:

– Where are you going?

– Jerusalem.

– Are you going to Palestine?

– Um, maybe. I don't know.

– You don't know. Are you going to the West Bank? To Gaza?

– Huh? Um, I don't know. I might tour around after Jerusalem. Gaza? I can go to Gaza?

– Hm. Where are you staying?

– With a friend in Jerusalem.

– Address?

– Urr, don't know. I have it in my bag, but my bag has been whisked away somewhere.

– How much money do you have?

– None.

– Dollars? Euros?

– None.

– How are you going to get to Jerusalem?

– Walking. It's free!

– Hm. How are you going to leave?

– I have money waiting for me in Jerusalem. Insh'Allah.

– Hm. Please go and sit in that pen over there for suspicious people.

Both of my new friends were also marked as suspicious as well as a Japanese guy. They also seemed to have no money either because we were all hungry all day. We waited. Other people joined the pen and left again a little later. We waited. I did some begging for food and got given a Snickers and a packet of biscuits so we all had a quarter each. We waited. After a few hours Kisar was taken away for interrogation, and he came back very shaken. After 5 hours Rita and Uki were called up to a desk where they were given a visa without any further question. Kisar had another interrogation and another, the last of which involved a strip search. He came trembling and unable to talk. Rita and Uki were going to walk with me to Jerusalem so they waited for me. Nothing, nothing, then a girl with ringlets gave me an interview.

– What is your religion?

– Christian.

– When you were in Syria did anyone try to convert you to Islam?

– Yes, all the time.

– Did you convert?

– Not exactly. You know that thing you say – “Lar Illih Illah Il’Allah, Muhammedan resull’allah”? Well I said that, and they seemed happy.

– You’re a Muslim then.

– Not really, no.

– What books do you have in your bag?

– Bible, Koran, Turkish dictionary.

– You have a Koran in your bag?

– Yes. It was a present.

– You brought it with you from England.

– No, someone gave it to me in Syria.

– Do you have a prayer mat?

– What? No. Look, I’m not a…

– How many times a day do you pray?

– Well I don’t, it depends…

– You don’t pray?

– Um, no, I do. Ur, once. I say a rosary, you know, the Catholic…

– What’s your Muslim name?

– Abdullah! Someone I met on the street…

– Abdullah. Sit in the pen, I'll examine your piece of paper.

Baffled, I sat back down. A little later, at 5pm, she took me to my bag so she could go through my stuff and take my address book and books to look at them. Rita and Uki said they'd wait till 5.30. I managed to cadge a loaf of bread and a croissant and I shared it with Rita but by this time I was battered by aggressive questioning, too little food, and too much time sitting and staring. Ringlets gave my books back and said, "Did you bring the Koran from England?" and I said, "No, it was a present." She said, "It is in English, you brought it from England with you." I couldn't understand why she was trying to prove that I was a Muslim or why I was becoming defensive about not being one. I still can't understand it: I watched Muslims come into Israel all day, it's not a problem. But she stated it as a fact – I had brought a Koran with me and I had lied about it. She also said it wouldn't be long before I got my passport. I was certainly pleased, but too exhausted to do a jig or anything.

One hour, two hours. I asked Ringlets if she thought I would get into Israel and she said, "No, I don't think so." My anxiety level rocketed upwards to Very Anxious. I did some pacing and some fidgeting.

At 7.30 in the evening I was told I wasn't allowed into Israel and would I please come this way. I said I wanted to speak to someone for an explanation. A surly police woman emerged from her office and in front of a queue of Palestinians said, "You have to leave Israel."

– Why?

– The Ministry of the Interior says you can't come in.

– Why?

– I can't tell you that.

– Can I speak to someone who can tell me?

– There's no one here who can tell you.

– No one? Wha?

– I'm sorry, this is not my decision.

– I've walked from Belgium to go to Jerusalem. 6 months.

– I understand. But you have to leave. You can go to the Ministry of the Interior in Amman and ask them.

– And they'll tell me why I can't come in?

– I'm sorry, there's nothing I can do for you.

– Will they let me have a visa?

– Maybe. You have to follow this man now.

– Gulp.

So I shakily put my finger on a fingerprint taker and blankly posed for a photo which presumably went onto their "Probable Muslims" list and I followed the security guy outside. He said, "Sit there," so I sat down next to another massive bunch of jostling Palestinians and I cried. Not the kind of manly crying you do when you watch *Life Is Beautiful* to prove you have emotions, but the childish kind of pure self-pity. I was at a pilgrimage-wide cheerfulness low of maybe 25% cheer. What in the heck do I do now?

Amman

My passport has a big red stamp in it which says in English, "Entry Denied," and in Hebrew, "Filthy Pig," so I think trying another border will not be worth my while, especially since I'll have to pay another fiver to get out again. So I decided to go to Amman to see if I can find the Ministry of the Interior. I anticipate a few days of zero fun, but I'm halfway there already and since I've never done anything anti-Israeli in my life I reckon they've got to change their minds and let me in. If they don't, I won't know what to do. I have a candle I've brought from Romania to light in the Orthodox church for the Gypsies. I have to pray for the baker family from Germany and that guy who gave me and Richard a loaf of sweetbread in Belgium. I have to go to Jerusalem. I was 30km away, one day's walk. They'll understand all that and they'll give me a visa. I mean, they have to, don't they?

Being a City Rat in Amman

August 10, 2009

Al Gore

Did I mention that when I was in Al Gore, the hottest place in the world, I met someone who insisted that I come and meet his friend who spoke English. I grudgingly agreed but said that I'd walk and he said, "No way, it's uphill, you have to drive." I thought maybe that if I insisted on walking enough the whole trip would get cancelled but instead he drove next to me in his car and I walked up a very steep hill and he kept saying, "Come on, get in." Eventually we got to his friend's house, very sweaty, and his friend had two portraits of Saddam Hussein on the wall. He said, "You love Saddam Hussein?" and I had to confess that I didn't.

To Amman

Here's a recap of my position a few days ago: Israel had turfed me out and drawn two big lines across my passport and told me that if I wanted a reason or to get a visa or anything I had to go to Amman to talk to the Ministry of the Interior, since it was their decision. Amman, luckily, is 500m further towards heaven than Al Gore so it stopped being so insanely hot, but it took me two days to get there and when I did get there I had nowhere to stay. The first thing I did was to go to the Israeli embassy which, being 5pm on a Thursday, was closed. The police who were guarding it told me that it would open again on Monday, a casual four days later. I'm afraid I swore at them, but they seemed to understand why and I apologised when I had regained my cool. My next plan was to find a place to sleep, so I hastily wrote to loads of people from couchsurfing saying I needed a bed tonight, and luckily one of them said I could stay with him. That was Kyle who I've been staying with since.

Killing Time

I found out that the British Embassy opens on Sunday so I thought I'd go there and see if they can do anything for me while I was waiting, but basically I've spent three days just killing time. I've explored in a lot of hotels which is quite a good way of entertaining oneself for free, and if the hotel is laid out right it can come with a bunch of free food as well. Yesterday I went up a 24-storey hotel onto the roof via the emergency exit stairwell. Because it's stairs and not a lift no one uses it, and because no one uses it there seems to be no security at all. So although the lift doesn't stop at several floors, like the 12th which is just a maze of ventilation shafts and such, the stairs have free access to everywhere. Even better, the stairs are next to the service lifts, so if you stop at every floor and pop your head through the first door, there's a bunch of leftovers sitting there, waiting to be thrown away. I had a weird meal of cold fishfingers and chips, fruit, croissants, nuts, Arabic sweets, two egg yolks, and cheese, all shoved into my mouth really fast in case someone turned up, and then I got onto the roof and looked across the whole city. It's not that pretty but I felt naughty and that makes it better.

Israeli Friendliness

On Sunday I walked three hours to the British Embassy and over a four minute chat they said, "I wish you well but there's nothing we can do. We don't interfere in other countries' immigration policies." Then I walked back. Today, Monday, I went to the Israeli embassy. There was a hoard of Palestinians or similar all being treated like cattle in the manner of the Israeli border, and a policeman shouting at them. I asked him where I should go and he looked at my passport and said, "Not here. British embassy. Go now." I stayed. Later, when he had a little more time, he said, "Go British embassy. No help you here." I stayed. Later I managed to speak to someone with slightly less time pressure who explained it like this: "You have two lines in your passport. They don't want you at the border, they don't want you in the consulate. We can't help you, they tell us if you have two lines…what colour are the lines?" he asked. I said, "Red." He snorted with laughter. "Ha! Yes, there's no chance. They won't see you. We can't let you in." I pointed out that they had told me at the border to come to the embassy for an explanation. He said, "They always say that. Whenever we have people with two red lines, there's nothing you can do. Go to your British embassy."

I'm at a loss

I think if I was one of those people who insisted on stuff and kicked up a fuss there might have been a way of seeing someone there, or even of just getting through the border in the first place. But officials and bureaucracy and such drain me very fast and if it's a choice between raising my voice or putting my tail between my legs and sitting under the table, I take the table option every time. So my two possible hopes in Amman have been tried and have failed. I don't know what to do now. I think I should try to get across the border illegally but I'm probably too much of a wuss. And I now have another problem – I don't even know how to get home. I suspect that Syria won't let me back in because of the Hebrew in my passport, not to mention the fact that I'd have to pay them loads again. If I'm right about that, I'm trapped between Israel who think I'm a Muslim and a load of Arab countries who'll think I'm a Jew. I guess I should sleep on it.

Waiting in Amman

August 12, 2009

More Loafing

I haven't got any more news to tell you really. A friend of a friend of a friend of a friend turns out to be the Israeli ambassador in Jordan or something and it seems just possible that this tenuous connection might be enough to get me a hearing or something where I can perhaps clear my name and my passport. A girl called Alex, who I haven't ever met or heard of, has written to people for me and started something moving though I don't know what. Now, entirely on the basis of this pretty small hope, I'm staying in Amman because it seems like the most useful place to be if I suddenly need to have an interview or something. In the meantime I'm walking around, exploring some hotels, talking to Kyle. Not quite nothing but it's on the borders of nothing.

My spirits, however, are high. I've quite recovered from the misery of a week ago and I've even done a couple of solids to celebrate. It's been particularly comforting to find that a whole bunch of my friends and family have been writing to me and offering useless advice and such.

Now for some more waiting.

Another Suspense-laden Instalment from Amman

August 19, 2009

Dead Sea

There's no question in my mind that you must be on tenterhooks. I can't think of a more appropriate use of the word in fact. And the reason you're on tenterhooks is because you want to know how I'm going to end up definitely getting to Jerusalem against all the odds in a miraculous manner. I'll tell you, but you're going to have to read an account of my holiday first. Since I was doing so much waiting around and since I didn't have any money, I thought I'd go on holiday to Petra and Aqaba. Aqaba's 300km away from Amman so I couldn't do it by walking, but who walks when they're on holiday? No one. So I set off by foot and decided that if anyone stopped and asked me if I wanted a lift, I'd accept. On the first day I got to the outskirts of Amman and stayed with a very interesting person who, among other things, had rejected Islam and tried to build a Green City and had studied all 300 or so religions and had experienced astral projection. He took me to the Dead Sea and told me that if you parked there for more than 15 minutes, the Israelis on the other side spot you from their satellites and they phone up the Jordanian police and tell them your coordinates and then they come along and hassle you. A point I mentally noted as relevant to my plan to swim across the Dead Sea.

Police Hospitality

In Petra I spent the night with the police because I was being arrested, I think. Well they never said I was being arrested but they certainly behaved like I was and they even tried to claim I'd broken some law. I discovered that Jordanian hospitality reaches its lowest ebb in the hands of the police. They gave me bread a few hours after I asked for it (I was on holiday so I didn't mind asking for food) and a falafel in the morning and let me sleep at 5.30 in the morning on the concrete yard outside the police station. They kept saying that it wasn't safe to sleep outside at night and after a while I came to the conclusion that their solution was to just keep me awake until it was day again.

Petra

Petra is a town which is made entirely of caves. It's totally incredible. These wingnut oldentimes guys must have arrived in this rocky desert and thought: If we just dig huge holes in these rocks then we can live in them! It's genius! And then it sort of became fashionable and the kings and such dug absolutely huge holes in the rocks. You can pay to get in and be among the tourists or you can go to a place called Little Petra which is effectively the suburbs and then you're all by yourself except for a couple of Bedouins who have sneaked into the caves to live there.

Bedouins

Speaking of which, I later met some Bedouins who are totally rad. They live in tents, that's part of the rules. But since tents are kind of a drag, lots of them have houses as well and some even live in the city, but they put a tent around the edge as a reminder. Anyway, these Bedouins I met, they were selling trinkets by the side of the road to tourists and they invited me in for tea, meal, bed. One of them told me that in the winter they go down into the valley where it's warmer and they do a bit of farming. Also drug smuggling. Apparently there's a market for drugs in Israel and Egypt and because it's hard to get across the border the Bedouins, who like dangerous work, rise to the challenge. It involves waiting till the wind gets up and, because of all the dust in the air, "if there's an Israeli soldier within even 3 metres of you, he can't see you." And they know the area pretty well so mostly it goes well for them, but sometimes one of them gets shot or has to shoot the Israeli soldiers. He has friends who are in jail for 15, 20 years and he made it sound as if it wasn't the kind of jail where you get a pool table and library. I asked him how long it would be if you crossed the border illegally but without drugs and he said maybe 3 months.

That's a relevant story because, combined with the other one about Israelis spying on me with satellites, it made me think that I'm just not up to the illegal crossing. I'm no Bedouin I suppose.

Aqaba

I went to Aqaba, that's a town I would happily not go to again but might end up in quite soon. Full of tourists and such. Someone pointed at a port and a bunch of houses and said, "They're knocking all this down. A sheik from the United Arab Emirates is building a complex here and they're moving the port down the coast". It's that kind of place. Small investigations led to the discovery that I can go to Egypt from there, which might be my only way home.

On the way back to Amman (where I am now) I decided to hitchhike for the first time in ages, with a sign and all. I got picked up by a truck driver who bought me three shawarmas and some bananas and orange juice. They have lots of conversations with each other while driving round here, conducted through the limited vocal range of the car horn, and the fruit of one of these conversations was that the truck that was driving past us stopped in front of us. We stopped too. They got out and lowered the ramps at the back so we could drive on. I was in a truck and we were being picked up by another truck. It was totally awesome except that the ramp was too steep or something so it didn't work.

Triumphal Entry

I may have mentioned that a friend's sister's friend's friend's dad is the Israeli ambassador in Jordan and that she'd asked her to ask her to ask him to ask him if he could help me and that it was possible that he would be able to. Get me legitimised or something. Well I haven't heard from him yet and honestly my hopes are fading. I cryptically mentioned that I might go back to Aqaba and I'll be more frank about it now: I think I might not ever get to Jerusalem. Soon I'm going to admit defeat, try to get to Egypt and then, I don't know, get on a boat or something back to Europe and hitchhike home.

But it's not quite defeat. Some mean people might think that Richard was kind of lame for dropping out of our pilgrimage before we even got out of Belgium but not me. Richard was solely responsible for the inspiration and initiation of this pilgrimage and consequently for a change of the course of my life and I don't want to make it seem like that was less essential than the middle bit that I've done by myself. But now it seems he might play another role as last-minute saviour. Here are some emails:

From: Richard
Date: Aug 11, 10:38pm

I want to help you get across the border. I could make my way down there on trains within a week. I want to do this. So say the word, and I will.

From: Mikey
Date: Aug 13, 3:15am

How about you finish it off? You could basically do the whole conclusion in the same way that you did the whole introduction. I'm suddenly quite excited by the idea. What do you think?

From: Richard
Date: Aug 13, 1:02pm

That's a very interesting offer. I would feel bad about being the one to do the last stretch, considering I let you down by bailing out so early. But if you'd rather me do it than no one do it, I'd like to do it, because I owe you a lot, and I agree it would in a sense be you, or us, completing our pilgrimage, in a sort of relay fashion, even though you did all the hard work. So…I'm going to try and get everything sorted as quickly as possible, and I'll make it my target to be there within 10 days.

I hope you can wait that long, and if you do get to Jerusalem by then, I'll meet up with you in there.

Richard

From: Richard
Date: Aug 14, 12:13am

OK. I'm going to be arriving at Queen Alia airport at 15:00 hours on Thursday the 20th August. It's all booked.

See you soon,
Richard

If you couldn't be bothered to read all that, the gist is that Richard's going to fly out here and hopefully take the baton for me and get to Jerusalem. Obviously he has to get past the Israeli border but I have accumulated a lot of border wisdom recently and I feel like I could tell Osama how to get through by now. First, shave that beard.

Richard in Amman

August 25, 2009

An email

I left you thinking, "What a massive loser, you can pretend you're 'finishing' the pilgrimage with the help of Richard if you like, but we all know that you've walked 5000km only to fail at the last moment." Which was a reasonably fair assessment. But what you didn't bank on was me getting this email:

From: Amit the Israeli
To: Mikey Lear
Date: Aug 20, 10:10

Michael Lear,

Please arrive at embassy on Tuesday morning at 8 a.m.

Amit,

The Israeli Embassy – Amman

Yes, that's right, I have friends on the inside and those friends have other friends and the result is that after a couple of weeks of waiting I have been actively summoned to the inner realms, the very place I was banned from until recently. The very place, in fact, where the people who could overturn the decision that was made against me were hiding. Summoned! Why would they summon me, right, unless they definitely wanted me to come into their country? What I naturally imagined and I'm sure you're imagining too, is a humble and penitent delegation of Israelis holding flowers and chocolates and novelty oversized cards saying, "We're sowwy," and the president or perhaps a stand-in assuring me of an armed escort to take me to Jerusalem.

And all I had to do was wait for another couple of days. So let me tell you what happened.

Richard

Richard arrived on the 20th which is the same time I got that email, so instead of us setting off straight away, we decided to wait for the fruit hampers because that way I could go to Jerusalem with him instead of him ditching me at the border. While waiting we have done a lot of important things like walking around, attempting to go on the roof of a hotel and getting rejected by a friendly security officer, making pancakes, meeting another guy who's staying with Kyle called Nathanael, frying bread and eating it with sugar, reading Noam Chomsky books and improving the world in general. Our plan was to get to the embassy at 8am on Tuesday, leave for Jerusalem at 8.45am with written apology and fresh visa in pocket.

Israeli Embassy

The police at the embassy, totally out of character, let me in without asking any questions. They didn't even ask to see my two red lines. The first stage was over with minimal difficulty by 9.30. Then I met some real Israelis, which was quite exciting, who said, "You need to go to the British embassy," which is a pretty standard lie, so I wasn't bothered by it and I showed them the printout of my email from Amit. They let me into the inner zone where a whole load of real Israelis dwelt. A small cluster of hours and one, "I'm sorry, there's nothing we can do, the Ministry of the Interior won't budge on this very serious issue" later and I was eyeball to eyeball with Amit. He obviously recognised that since he'd invited me there it would have been a bit rich to say the same thing, so instead he said, "Well we're going to have to write a letter to the Ministry of the Interior about your case, and they may change their minds. But it'll take a couple of weeks, maybe three." Delightedly I said, "Great! Only three weeks of waiting! Joy! So, do you think they'll let me in then?" and he said, "Maybe." On further pushing he admitted that it would be a minimum of one week and there was a 50% chance that they'd change their minds.

50%

50%. That's not a huge % to risk a three week (estimated) wait on. Plus it was a prediction made by someone who is an expert in getting people to leave his building but I saw how he dealt with this Jewish guy in front of me in the queue (British and thinking of moving to Israel), and it was much less friendly. My conclusion is that I still have a smouldering ember of hope left. In the meantime I'm going to give my stick, candle, and list of people to pray for to Richard, walk with him (and Nathanael, who seems to have some spare time) to the border, and then come back and chill.

To the Israeli Border (again)

August 29, 2009

Passport Hilarity

On Wednesday afternoon (not quite the early morning we'd planned – faffing time goes up considerably with more people) we headed for the King Hussein Bridge again, back down the 30km hill I'd climbed up a few weeks ago. Some way down the hill Richard noticed that the jacket which had been resting on top of his rucksack wasn't there. While Nathanael and I were thinking to ourselves, "I hope he can't be bothered to go and look for it," Richard made the further discovery that his passport had been in the pocket of the jacket. As far as he was concerned, that was a clincher and he resolved to find it. We set off back up the hill, retracing our steps and carefully examining the ground in case the jacket had got hidden under a pile of leaves or something. It hadn't. It was just lying on the pavement, not far away from Kyle's house where we'd started and very far from the spot down the hill where we'd walked to. So a certain amount of extra walking was added and the only bonus was that Nathanael sensibly took a photograph of Richard looking glum standing next to me holding my passport and looking happy.

Animal Welfare

Then on Thursday (after spending a cheerful night in a church – Nathanael hadn't got a sleeping bag and none of us had a tent) we covered the remaining ground to the border which was, in an unlikely manner, open. I spoke to Richard before about him possibly becoming a vegetarian. He had some old-fashioned idea that by eating meat you were in some way partly responsible for them being killed and he didn't like the thought of that, but then he didn't like the thought of not eating meat either so he was in a bit of conflict. While we were walking down a hill we saw a sight that was, for Richard, life-changing. That sight was the ordinary workings of a small halal slaughter house which bizarrely had its door open to the road and, consequently, to us.

We stopped and stared for a bit at the various processes they were using to fleece, gut, hang, clean and butcher about 20 lambs. Having seen an artisan lamb slaughter, I was fairly unimpressed. Pneumatic syringes were used to inflate the sheep so the fleece would come off more easily, whereas the Bulgarian master had peeled it off with his fingers; the guts were bundled together and shipped off to somewhere else while the Bulgarian had had an intimate knowledge of every organ; the workers had the slouch of the man who is paid by the hour and who doesn't mind if blood gets on the wool and all in all it just seemed a little dreary. However they told us that if we waited for five minutes we'd get to see the actual killing of a cow and although Richard probably would have voted for moving on, me and Nathanael felt we could spare the time and we stayed. It was pretty horrific.

Maybe most people know what a cow being killed looks like but I didn't so I'm going to describe it for the benefit of anyone else who might be as ignorant as me. After dragging it in, which they didn't find easy (R and N both later claimed that they could see the fear in the bull's eyes – personally I thought it was behaving like bulls always do, which is stupidly), they knocked its feet from under it so it was lying down and cut its throat. Up till then the bulls resistance had been mostly practical – it was trying to get away from the people who were pushing it around – and for a few moments as the blood filled the floor it carried on in this manner which was silent. Then it started mooing out of desperation. Only after a decent amount of blood had gone, but once it started mooing it didn't stop for a while. And when I say mooing, I don't mean mooing in the traditional sense because that requires that the throat is attached to the mouth. This mooing was coming through the voice box so it was loud and recognisably a moo, but then out of the throat so it was a sort of coarse and hollow bray, the sort which doesn't occur in nature but does occur in horror films probably.

It started mooing after its throat had been cut and I thought, "That's the sound of agony. Kill it properly. Kill it now, it's horrible," but they didn't need me to think that because they were going to do it anyway. After the blood was all on the floor they carried on cutting the neck until the head was off. The braying continued. The bull could take a full breath and then groan it all out several times without a head. The legs were flailing away as well. A minute went by without pause in the kicking or mooing. Another minute and there was a pause. The head, which had been set on the stump of its neck, open its mouth slowly while its dislocated eyes gave away nothing of what it was trying to say. Then it closed its mouth and that was about two minutes after decapitation. The legs started up again. More groaning, the kicking became more sporadic, the groaning got a little quieter and then suddenly back to full volume. After five minutes there was little enough movement for them to start work on the body, although even as they pulled it round I saw a muscle contract.

Afterwards I asked Richard if he really thought five minutes of fairly gruesome death was worth giving up meat for and he said, "I'm a vegetarian." I asked him, "You mean you're not going to eat beef now?" and he said grimly, "That's it. I'm a vegetarian". Later I offered him some bread and he asked me if it had any gelatine in it.

Vigil

I'm now back in Amman and continuing my vigil. Is it a vigil when you just wait around for ages for no reason? That's what I'm continuing anyway. Hopefully Richard and Nathanael will reach Jerusalem tomorrow, but for all I know they got rejected by the Israelis and are on their way back here. Richard is armed with my stick, the candle from

Romania and a list of people I said I'd pray for in Jerusalem. His return flight is from Amman so hopefully I'll see him before he goes back home.

Richard in Jerusalem

August 31, 2009

From: Richard
To: Mikey
Date: Sat, Aug 29

The border crossing went pretty well. Nathanael got through like a breeze while I was questioned on many things, and stopped and re-questioned. It wasn't too bad though, and they never took my stuff or left me waiting. We were then forced to get a bus a couple of miles to drop us off outside the gates of the border area (if we'd attempted to walk out, we'd have been shot, apparently). Then we walked a few miles that night and slept in open desert near the road. The following day was really hot, and we spent a large chunk of it in an Israeli haven restaurant in the middle of nowhere, but got a goodly amount of walking done in the morning and evening. Then we approached some Bedouins, telling them we were looking for a place to sleep, and they had us sit round their fire, made us sugary tea, chatted, then we slept in two bug-ridden mattresses which resulted in insane itching all night long and virtually no sleep. Then this morning we pushed on to Jerusalem. I've already had a look at the Holy Sepulchre, but I haven't prayed or lit candles for your gypsies yet, but the pilgrimage is essentially complete now. So, here's to that.

Oh, and also we bumped into that Luke guy in the street in Jerusalem. He and that Brazilian girl were apparently kept for 8 hours at the border. Nathanael and me are clearly liked by

Jews. Also, we've seen a lot of Orthodox Jews, and one told Nathanael off for using a camera on the Sabbath, and many Jewish schoolchildren throw things at cars for driving on the Sabbath.

Richard

The End of the Pilgrimage

September 2, 2009

Israel Speaks

From: consul-assist <consul-assist@amman.mfa.gov.il>
To: Mikey Lear
Date: Wed, Sep 2, 2009 at 9:08 AM

Dear Mikey,

I'm very sorry to inform you that your appeal request was denied.

I wish for you only the best at the rest of your trip.

Amit Djerassi – Israeli Embassy, Amman

****
This footnote confirms that this email message has been scanned by PineApp Mail-SeCure for the presence of malicious code, vandals & computer viruses.
****

My Wait is Over

I just got this email and my first reaction was, "Oh good, there are no viruses or vandals in this email," but then I looked at the bit that Amit had written and I saw that there was also some bad news. Now I need a plan. Right, I've thought of one. Richard has completed our pilgrimage and sent me a picture of my stick in Jerusalem to prove it and that's good enough for me. Now it's time to go home. I've got more than 150 Euros in my pocket so I should be able to at least get out of Jordan and pay the fine I've accrued for my overdue visa. Who knows, there may be some left over to buy myself some bread or something.

So, for the optimistic slash generous: We've finished our pilgrimage and I'm blazing home in glory. For the cynical slash realistic: We've both given up on our pilgrimages in different ways and I'm slinking home in shame. For the pilgrimage purist, this is the end.

Getting Home – Egypt

September 7, 2009

Leaving Jordan

Here's my plan: Amman – Aqaba – Egypt – Libya – Some other countries – Morocco – Spain – and you can guess the rest. 800km a day and a few extra days for unforeseen circumstances and I'll be home in a couple of weeks. Well this is how I started. Getting down to Aqaba, across the sea to Egypt and up to Alexandria was the work of two days. I cunningly used the night to cross the sea, saving time and meaning that I got a free night's sleep. 'Free' in that I paid quite a lot of my 200 Euros for the whole thing and 'sleep' in that I slept on various floors, decks and benches for small stretches of time in each. But I was moving and that was definitely good.

To Greece

In Alexandria I investigated the possibility of getting a boat from there directly to Europe, cutting out the middle man of those other North African countries. It seems that legitimate ferries have been suspended for a while now but I luckily made friends with a man who worked in the cargo port who presented me with the possibility of crossing to Greece illegally in a container ship. The way he said it he made it sound like there was literally no danger of anything bad happening at all, so I became persuaded. The plan was he'd take me past the port police in his car and do some bribing (he needed 300 Egyptian pounds for the purposes of bribery; not for him, he was quite clear, but for bribing the others). Then he'd put me in an empty container and close the door and I'd hand over 150 of the pounds. Then I'd wait (but I'd be able to open the door from the inside because you can when the containers are empty) and after a few hours I'd be hoiked into the container pile. Then I'd wait some more (he stressed the importance of taking water with me) and the ship would start moving. Then I'd wait for maybe 24 hours and we'd arrive in some place in Greece I'd never heard of. Then I'd wait till the containers were all unloaded, wait a little more to be sure the coast was clear, and then I'd just amble out after giving the other 150 pounds to some other guy (this part of the plan was less clear). And if I saw any police I was to present them with sheesha tobacco and say, "This is a gift from Egypt" and they would be sure to kiss me on both cheeks and not to ask for my passport. That was the plan as it was outlined and I accepted.

Jimmy

After escorting me to various travel agencies to establish the non-existence of my other options, all the time pointing out how people were saying, "Hello" to him and that that proved he was a good person, we went to a bank because I was a little short of Egyptian pounds. I should mention that the total price of this enterprise in English money was going to be about 45 quid, assuming I didn't end up in jail with a big fine. Just before we got to the bank he stopped me, handed me some sort of ID card and asked for the money so he could change it for me. I said, "No thanks, I'll do it myself," and he appeared to take umbrage. Still, he was anxious to maintain

English-Egyptian relations so he put up with my little slight. In the bank, after a little struggle, he managed to prise my money out of my hand and he changed it for me. I kept my beady eyes on him and it seemed like I got the right amount of money back, however my obvious distrust was beginning to upset him. The next stop was the sheesha shop where I managed to persuade him that I didn't want 10 packets but only 5 and I had to be quite forceful to be able to pay for them myself. And he still took the change for me and then counted it into my hand. By this stage my distrust level had gone up and his umbrage levels had gone up also. Did I mention that his name was Ahmed in Egyptian or Jimmy in English, and that he was slightly paralysed on one side? I should have because the last time I took against someone for having a gammy arm, he turned out to be really nice so I was well disposed to Jimmy from the start. Especially since his paralysis made him dribble constantly, although in retrospect it could have been the prospect of ripping me off that caused that.

We went to a café to meet his accomplice in human trafficking and we took our third taxi. When he said, "You pay" I started to suspect that something was possibly rotten in Denmark, even though I really wanted to believe that he was just a friendly crook who wanted to help me out in one of the coolest ways anyone has ever tried to help me. But making me pay for a taxi? Well, there's a limit. In the café I decided not to have a tea this time because I could see the way things were going. So I watched Jimmy drink his and then he said, "I've got 60 pounds but I need another 40 so I can go and bribe the police." That seemed a bit rich. I was meant to pay him when I was on the boat, not in a café, and I said as much. This, in his eyes, was an outright demonstration of bad faith, and he said as much also. I think he raised his voice. I pointed out that I was quite scared and he went too far – he questioned my masculinity. By this stage I had spent 45 Egyptian pounds (about 8 quid or something) on sheesha tobacco so I was pretty heavily invested in the plan, but when I'm asked, "Are you a boy or a man?" I feel obliged to take serious action. I said, "Half and half," and as I was thinking, "Maybe I should just cut my losses and bail" I noticed the guy behind the bar was catching my eye and shaking his head ominously. That was enough for me and I pulled out of our venture, but Jimmy thought that I owed him for the time he'd wasted trying to con me. Outside the café we created a spectacle which gathered a small crowd. He was shouting at me that I owed him 25 pounds for various imagined reasons (the tea, the taxis, some sort of commission on the money he changed for me in the bank) and insisting that we go to the police. The crowd were in favour of me just paying up because after all, it was only 3 Euros. When I refused they said I should just go to the police and that would be the end of it, but I was quite rattled by Jimmy's certainty. I thought maybe he was chums with the police or something. Well I didn't know what to think. Voices were being raised. It was confusing. In the end I went with him to the police station and it turned out to be a pretty bold bluff. As we were walking along he came up with more and more implausible threats, ending with, "You'll go to prison for three years for trying to sneak into a cargo boat," by which time I'd stopped replying to him. He didn't follow me into the police station, and that was how I dealt with the menace of Jimmy.

When I was pretty sure he'd gone I went back to the café to say thank you to the bar man. He met me on the street and said, "Jimmy's in there. He said you paid him." Well that's what you get for trusting someone who dribbles.

A Night in Alex

Wandering around in Alex (as they call it here) some old guy spotted me and asked if I wanted to stay at his house. I said, "Yes," naturally, and when I got there I noticed that he didn't have anything. Some basic furniture, but no clothes, no cutlery, no food, no pen, no lighter. It was almost as if he didn't live there. Then he gave me a key and said, "Will you be going out?" I assured him that I would not be leaving my valuables alone where he could get his conman's hands on them and he smiled amiably and left me to it. It turned out that he was renovating the apartment and living in another one and that he didn't have any intention of robbing me. In fact, he gave me a couple of sandwiches and was thoroughly nice.

Ghadaffi

I hitched to Libya the next day, found that I should have got a visa before I arrived at the border and headed back to Cairo. That's a small detour of 600km or a day's hitchhike to me. That's where I am now, having had a proper Iftar with a family like you're meant to in Ramadan. Oh, it's Ramadan. Did I mention that? Well I'll expound the hilarious implications another time. Tomorrow I'll encounter more bureaucrats from the pocket of Ghadaffi, the wacky funster, and I'm slightly anticipating bad news. I wish I knew how to bribe people, I'm sure that would be the answer.

Waiting in Cairo

September 12, 2009

An Attempt on Libya

The Libyan border gave me the impression that Libya runs on bribes. No one specifically said, "Give me a bribe now," but there was quite a lot of holding my passport and slowly examining it by different officials before I was kicked out of the country and I may be wrong but I suspect that if I'd had some spare cash and known how to discreetly palm it into someone's palm, I could have got through. But that didn't happen, so I went back to Cairo with the instructions that I could get a visa from there.

Luckily I was picked up by Ahmed who not only was going to Cairo but also was happy to let me stay at his house and even was happy to drive me around the next day and wait in embassies, which isn't everyone's idea of fun. First the Libyan embassy, who apparently said that my passport (which is English and written in English) was too English. Ideally it would be Arabic, but since I had to make do with what I'd got, they'd accept a translation of it if I got one from the British embassy. And after that I'd need a passport photo and then it would be a two- to four-week wait for the visa. Another slight whiff of bribe-me was wafting round the room. We went to the British Embassy and they said, "Here's the form you have to fill in, and it'll cost you 105 pounds and the translation will be ready tomorrow morning." At that point I decided not to bother with Libya. 105 Egyptian pounds is only about 15 English pounds, but I can't hear an amount which sounds so big without feeling a little pale. And that was just for permission to wait for "two to four weeks" and then probably be rejected by Libya (the Hebrew in my passport, it seems, says, "Not welcome almost anywhere"). So I cut my losses at having paid £2.50 for 12 passport photos (which came with a free postcard-sized print of me looking grim and passporty, surrounded by pink flowers and hearts and framed) and pinned my hopes on getting to Cyprus by boat.

After a whole bunch of fruitless research I eventually managed to book a one-way ticket on a cruise to Cyprus (that's a cruise, not a ferry – and in case you're too plebby to know what the difference is, I think food is included in a cruise and it costs more) but that leaves on Tuesday. Which left me with a whole bunch of waiting to do in Cairo. I've spent most of that waiting time at Rafik's house (he's from couchsurfing), hiding from the world.

Perfume and Papyrus

When I first got here I had to go and do some shopping and since I didn't know my way around I couldn't effectively pull off the eyes-to-the-floor-tight-lipped-hussle which stops people from chatting to you if you look foreign. One of these people shook my hand and said, "Where you from, friend?"

and he didn't let go for a while. A bad sign, I find. "Ah, England. I like English. I know York, Birmingham, Manchester." Lots of smiling and friendliness from this guy. "I'll give you my card." People give me their cards quite a lot which I normally think of as an olive branch but smaller and more convenient. I have a bag full olive branches and a pocket full of other more crumpled olive branches. He pulled me towards somewhere I wasn't going, and I raised an eyebrow. "Just round the corner, my shop." And he smiled at me in a confused sort of way as if to say that it was such an obviously good idea to follow him that it was a little bit quaint that I was resisting. In his shop, which had perfume bottles all over the walls, I was told to sit down without being offered a business card. I sat. Then I was offered tea. I also had a suspicion that I was about to experience the Hard Sell, and I was not disappointed. "You have a wife? Girlfriend? Hm. This very nice. Smell." I became slightly impatient and I think he noticed. "Only two pounds, very cheap. Smell – one bottle is ok, okay?" I became very clear at this point that I wasn't going to buy any perfume. "Why not?" he said. After he'd eventually admitted defeat he said, in a resigned and deflated manner, "Then I'll just show you some papyrus then." No, I did not want papyrus, possibly I have even less use for papyrus than for perfume which is none at all. No papyrus, please. Normally in these kinds of situations I wait to be excused before I leave but I got the impression that he would have kept me there all day, so I got up and left.

A little bit later, and with a fairly heavy bag of shopping, I met someone else who also took an instant shine to me. "Ah! England. I know England a little. I have been to York. I'll give you my business card." Naturally I squinty-eyed him a little bit for saying exactly the same thing as the guy from a few hours ago, but he did a face of total innocence and wonder, so I said, "OK, let me have your card," and held my hand out. He looked at me as if I was crazy and then led me towards his shop. At the door I started to put up a bit of resistance, partly because I felt a bit like I'd been through this before and partly because I literally had been through this exact door before, and the previous shyster was sitting outside smiling at me as if he hadn't tried to rip me off and as if his brother wasn't trying to do the same. I pointed all this out to my new chum and he waved it aside as if it were a road marking (which are very conscientiously ignored by everyone here – the driving is absolutely mental). Once again I found myself inside the perfume shop and being told to sit down – but I had a card up my sleeve. "Where's the business card?" I said. "You want to smell this?" "Could I just have the business card?" "Mmmm [ecstatically, and as if for the first time] rose! Aaaah. Smell!" "No, I'll just take your card and go." "Yes, of course, how about this one?" "Sorry, do you have a business card or not?" "A moment…have a look at this papyrus." "I'm absolutely not going to buy any papyrus, but I'd like to have your business card please." "Yes, of course, papyrus is a good souvenir though, just have a look." And then I shouted, "NO!" at him. And then I apologised and said, "Thank you," and he just looked at me and waited for me to go. "Could I have your card then?" He waved apologetically at his desk as if he'd done a thorough search and only managed to find the empty business card box and a post-it saying, "Get more business cards ASAP," and that was it. Well, almost. Before I'd got back to Rafik's house a couple of teenagers said to me, "Ahh, England, my father has been to York, you want to eat with me tonight? Come, I'll give you my card." I had to put all my effort into not ending up in there a third time but he got me to the door and he was so limpet-like I had to walk away from him while he was still talking to me.

Later an old man offered to give me his business card and I said, "No. I HATE business cards." and walked off. I'm becoming such a badass.

Religious Birthmarks

On the ferry to Egypt I talked to someone with a big awkward brown birthmark thing on his forehead. I stared at it for a bit when I thought he wasn't looking but I didn't comment because that might have been rude. Then a bit later I saw someone else with a similar thing and I thought maybe it wasn't a birthmark but some kind of branding, like they were both in a gang or were criminals of a particular nature or something. And now I've seen loads of them all over the place and it turns out that the official explanation is that they are bruises you get from praying a lot: you know, when you bow down to Allah and put your forehead on that special little carpet you have to carry around with you to stop your forehead from bruising; that's when you get the bruises. The weird thing is that I didn't see any of these bruises in Turkey or Syria or Jordan. Only in Egypt, and here they're everywhere. Perhaps they have very hard carpets here.

Getting Home

September 23, 2009

Egypt to Cyprus

You presumably have never been on a cruise and you never intend to go on one, so I'll tell you what it's like. It's like going on a ferry but the meals are included in the price (which is bigger). So it's like going on a ferry and buying expensive meals. Also, if you go on a cruise by yourself then you have to sit on a special losers-table-for-one in the restaurant where everyone can see that you've taken two puddings to compensate for your lack of friends. On the plus side, I made it to Cyprus which is in Europe. People in Cyprus drink alcohol, they wear their hair out in public even if they're a girl, they eat food in the street in Ramadan and they generally behave like English people. In fact most of them are English. That was nice for me, being a little England-starved as I was, but not as nice as actually getting home, so I went across to the Turkish side to get a ferry to Turkey. Something I didn't know about Cyprus is that it is a country of its own and it is split down the middle by a green line where UN troops hang out and stop the northerners from bothering the southerners. The south is Greek and the north is Turkish and they don't really like each other very much. The Greek Cypriot policeman at the green line (which goes right through the middle of capital, Nicosia) asked me if I was going to "the occupied territories," and I said, "Yes, I'm going to the northern part." He said, "No, we call it 'the occupied territories' here. You see the Turkish have invaded our country and stolen our homes from us," and I slightly guiltily said, "Um, yes, then I'm going to the occupied territories." Although the Turkish bit is in the north, so I was right the first time too.

Cyprus to Turkey

Despite the tourist information and travel agencies in the south telling me there was no way to exit Cyprus by boat and that I'd have to fly, there is actually a regular ferry service going from the north to Turkey about 3 times a day. When I asked the Greeks if I could maybe, possibly, in the case of an emergency, get out of Cyprus from the north they just shrugged and said, "Dunno. Whatever." Although there's not much killing and violence going on, there's still quite a feeling that everything you say is politically loaded.

After I paid for the ticket, got to Turkey, bought another Turkish visa, paid a mystery €5 tax to a guy in a booth and got to an area where I wouldn't need any more visas, I had €10 left. That was on Friday night and over the next four and a half days I squandered the whole lot on food. By Sunday night I had hitched to the Bulgarian border with Turkey, so I left Muslim territory just at the end of Ramadan. It would have been disappointing to leave before then because on Eid/Bayram (which is the Muslim version of Easter) they celebrate by giving away sweeties at petrol stations.

Turkey to England

On Monday I waited by the border for half a day thinking, "Gru. This is going to take ages and I want to get home." But then a Turkish guy with an English number plate saw my sign which said LONDON and he thought, "I'm going to London, and furthermore, this guy could do some map reading for me." He was not wrong. We belted it across Europe stopping only to: pay the Serbians £100 for special Serbia-insurance (Shah only had Europe-insurance which obviously didn't include Serbia); have our car thoroughly searched by the Serbians (this stopped after half an hour because Shah had the brilliant idea of giving them two packets of cigarettes); sleep for four hours; pay a €150 fine to Slovenia for not buying a motorway card; swap drivers; pay tolls and buy petrol (loads of money); and get on a ferry to Dover. We arrived in England at 1.30 on Wednesday morning when we parted ways, me to a tent in a churchyard and Shah to London. This morning I hitched on home.

The End

And so there you have it: on the 19th of January 2009 I set off from Brussels with Richard with the aim of walking to Jerusalem with no money. After a couple of weeks Richard had a change of heart and went home and then I walked for the next six months until I reached Israel where I was denied entry into the country, no explanation given, and Richard flew out to Amman and completed out pilgrimage. He reached Jerusalem on August the 29th and I returned home alone.

Awards

Most Generous Country: Romania
Least Generous Country: Austria
Biggest Alcohol Drinkers: Hungarians
Biggest Tea Drinkers: Turkey
Warmest Country: Syria
Coldest Country: Austria
Dirtiest Countries: Syria and Romania
Most Precise Road Signs: Germany
Least Precise Road Signs: Syria

Least Connected Country (to the internet): Syria
Second Least Connected Country: Germany
Richest Country: Austria
Poorest Country: Romania
Best Food: Austria (because everything tastes good when you're really hungry)
Least Favourite Country: Israel
Favourite Countries: Turkey, Romania and Hungary
Hottest Place: Jordan Valley
New Addresses in My Address Book: 400
Money Stolen: €30
Money Spent: $100 on visas (some was given unprompted, some I begged for)
Dog Bites: 2 (minor)
Most Number of People on One Motorbike: 6 in Syria
Hours in the Israeli border: 9
Total Emotional Breakdowns: 1
Total Time Attempting to Get Into Israel: 1 month
Distance Walked: 5,000km or 3,000miles
Days Walked: About 200

And that's about it.

Mikey Lear lives in Barcombe Cross,
East Sussex, where he may or may not be
running a café in his garden shed.

Lightning Source UK Ltd.
Milton Keynes UK
05 June 2010

155149UK00001B/14/P

9 780956 422217